AF568056

THE GREAT SANCTIONS HACK

THE GREAT SANCTIONS HACK

URJIT PATEL

RUPA

Published by
Rupa Publications India Pvt. Ltd 2025
161-B/4, Gulmohar House,
Yusuf Sarai Community Centre,
New Delhi 110049

Sales centres:
Bengaluru Chennai
Hyderabad Kolkata Mumbai

P-ISBN: 978-93-7003-261-3
E-ISBN: 978-93-7003-759-5

First impression 2025

10 9 8 7 6 5 4 3 2 1

Printed in India

For my mother,
and
for the benefit of sanctioners

CONTENTS

LIST OF ABBREVIATIONS

AIIB	Asian Infrastructure Investment Bank
BBC	British Broadcasting Corporation
BRI	Belt and Road Initiative
BRICS	Brazil, Russia, India, China, South Africa group
CAC	Capital Accountability Convertibility
CFETS	China Foreign Exchange Trade System
CFSP	Common Foreign and Security Policy
CIBM	China Interbank Bond Market
CIPS	Cross-border Interbank Payment System
CMIC	Chinese Military-Industrial Complex Companies
CNN	Cable News Network
CTBT	Comprehensive Test Ban Treaty
DUP	Directly Unproductive Profit-seeking
EEAS	European External Action Service
EIA	Energy Information Administration
EU	European Union

FMCBG	Finance Ministers and Central Bank Governors
GFC	Global Financial Crisis
GSDB	Global Sanctions Data Base
G7	Group of Seven
G20	Group of Twenty
IAEA	International Atomic Energy Agency
IAMs	Integrated Assessment Models
IEA	International Energy Agency
IMF	International Monetary Fund
INSTEX	Instrument in Support of Trade Exchanges
IOC	International Oil Company
JCPOA	Joint Comprehensive Plan of Action
NATO	North Atlantic Treaty Organization
NDB	New Development Bank
NIOC	National Iranian Oil Company
NIPFP	National Institute of Public Finance and Policy
NPT	Nuclear Non-Proliferation Treaty
NSG	Nuclear Suppliers Group
ODA	Official Development Assistance
OFAC	Office of Foreign Assets Control (US)
OPEC	Organization of Petroleum Exporting Countries
PBOC	People's Bank of China
RMB	Renminbi
SAFE	State Administration of Foreign Exchange
SDR	Special Drawing Rights
SHFE	Shanghai Futures Exchange
SMIC	Semiconductor Manufacturing International Corporation

STFM	System for Transfer of Financial Messages
SWIFT	Society for Worldwide Interbank Financial Telecommunication
TIES	Threat and Imposition of Sanctions dataset
TOT	Terms of Trade
UAE	United Arab Emirates
UK	United Kingdom
UN	United Nations
US	United States of America
WDR	World Development Report
WEO	World Economic Outlook
WTO	World Trade Organization

PREFACE

PRIOR TO 2022, I paid as much attention to the subject of sanctions as I did to news of meteor showers. In other words, I ignored both.

My benign indifference ended in early 2022, when I joined the Asian Infrastructure Investment Bank (AIIB) at roughly the same time as the outbreak of the Ukraine-Russia war. Without exaggeration, between February and September 2022, no meeting at AIIB in which I participated was without a major discussion on the spectre of secondary sanctions on the Bank. Russia's shareholding in AIIB was the root cause.

At the time, there was a clear and present danger that a single country's shareholding in a multilateral bank with about a hundred members could invite severe and binding secondary sanctions by Western countries—many of whom were themselves shareholders in AIIB. Had this come to pass, the Bank's access to global capital markets would have been seriously circumscribed. Eventually, wise counsel prevailed in the important capitals of the world, and a bullet was avoided.

At a personal level, this episode sparked my curiosity on the topics of sanctions, secondary sanctions, countersanctions, and countermeasures. *The Great Sanctions Hack* is the culmination of this research endeavour, undertaken at the behest of Vijay Kelkar, a longstanding mentor. In my limited experience, I have noticed that publishers, as a rule, prefer long books—tomes. I countered this by paraphrasing Blaise Pascal: I would have written a longer book had I not had the time, but wrote a shorter one because I had all the time in the world.

I started working on the book in April 2024. The early 'harvest' was published as National Institute of Public Finance and Policy (NIPFP) Working Paper #421 in November 2024; the project was completed in August 2025. The views expressed here are personal and should not be attributed to NIPFP, or to anyone else, in any manner.

I am grateful to Gunjan Bhojwani for excellent research assistance. Rahool Pai-Panandiker was a first-rate sounding board; I am indebted to him. I am thankful to Sacchidananda Mukherjee, Prashant Girbane, Rohit Dutt, Jennifer Dadrewala, Yashpal Charan, Ashutosh Raravikar, Andre Charan, Narendra Jadhav, Anupama Roy and Dibakar Ghosh. I owe immense gratitude to Yoto V. Yotov and his colleagues at the LeBow College of Business, Drexel University for sharing the Global Sanctions Data Base, which they make available to all researchers; they were also kind to issue my working paper, 'Asphyxiation by Sanctions: Harm, Fear and Smog', at the Center on Global Policy Analysis.

Roberto Zagha and the late Meghnad Desai provided much encouragement. Richard Baldwin has been magnanimous in allowing me to usurp part of the title of his book.

1

PROLIFERATION WITHOUT DIMINUTION[1]

Time will tell if we are in an era of war, but, undoubtedly, we are in the era of economic sanctions.[2]

THE CURRENT CENTURY has witnessed a deluge of economic sanctions, with the attendant entropy. Few will

---

1 Chapters 1, 2 and 5 are based on my working paper issued as Patel, Urjit R., 'Asphyxiation by Sanctions: Harm, Fear and Smog', *Working Paper 421*, National Institute of Public Finance and Policy, New Delhi, 2024; *CGPA Working Paper 2025-06*, Center for Global Policy Analysis, LeBow College of Business, Drexel University, 2025.

2 Apparently, sanctions (or embargoes) have been around for millennia. The Megarian Decree in 432 BC is one of the earliest chronicled cases, when Megarians were proscribed from using the ports and markets of Athens.

disagree that the scale of sanctions has contributed to global economic disorder, and that their overhang, conceivably, has been a factor in vitiating the investment climate. If one were to summarise in a sentence the disquisitions on economic sanctions, it could be the following: if war is the pursuit of diplomacy by other means, economic sanctions are an instrument to inflict damage by an alternative agency.[3]

Sanctions are akin to laying a slow-burning siege. Wars are waged to exact direct physical destruction; economic sanctions and associated extraterritorial instruments are, in the first place, wrought to engender direct economic *harm*, and eventually indirect material damage, including to human capital. Qualitatively, the final intent is not different. And the underlying instrumentality is the same: harm and fear.[4]

In 2025, the arsenal has considerably broadened to include (generalised) secondary *tariffication*—threats by the US to impose tariffs on third-country targets for (purely) non-economic objectives, such as foreign and security policies (India) and domestic political factors (Brazil and South Africa). It has been argued, with justification, that wide-ranging cross-border economic curbs have increasingly been a subterfuge for pursuing mercantilist trade and investment policies against foreign national champions. For the most part, I have kept this frame of reference outside the purview of the book.

---

3 Baldwin, David A., *Economic Statecraft*, Princeton University Press, Princeton, NJ, 1985; and Blackwill, Robert D., and Jennifer M. Harris, *War by Other Means: Geoeconomics and Statecraft*, Harvard University Press, Cambridge, MA, 2016.

4 Using the term *violence* instead of *harm* may come across as emotional, hence is eschewed.

To use a central banking terminology, the impact on *current* and *potential* output of an economy, compared to a conflict-free base path, is felt almost instantaneously in a military war, but with sanctions, the sanctioned country's national balance sheet is degraded over time. The weakening of the target then leads to a change in military production.[5]

The literature is forthright that economic sanctions—curbs on trade and shipping, banking, payment channels, capital markets, insurance and conditions on the assets and liabilities of multilateral development banks—are a substitute for military war for lining up diplomatic agendas (see **Table 1.1**). Moreover, a negative narrative, combined with the threat of sanctions, carries the risk of undermining confidence and provoking a speculative attack on a country's currency.

5 Pape, Robert A., 'Why Economic Sanctions Do Not Work', *International Security*, vol. 22, 1997, pp. 90–136.

Table 1.1: Goals for Sanctions, 2000–2023

Objective of sanctioners	Number of sanctions
End War	167
Prevent War	82
Terrorism	121
Policy Change#	165
Destabilise Regime	11
Human Rights*	274
Democracy*	218

#This includes nuclear proliferation.
*There is overlap; sanctioners seek more than one concession from the target with the same set of sanctions.
Source: Global Sanctions Database (GSDB-R4);[6] *Felbermayr et al., 2020;*[7] *Yalcin et al., 2025*[8]

6 Global Sanctions Data Base (GSDB-R4), LeBow College of Business, Drexel University, 2025.

7 Felbermayr, Gabriel J., Aleksandra Kirilakha, Constantinos Syropoulos, Erdal Yalcin, and Yoto V. Yotov, 'The Global Sanctions Data Base', *European Economic Review*, vol. 129, 2020, pp. 1–23.

8 Yalcin, Erdal, Gabriel Felbermayr, Heider Kariem, Aleksandra Kirilakha, Ohyun Kwon, Constantinos Syropoulos, and Yoto V. Yotov, 'The Global Sanctions Data Base—Release 4: The Heterogeneous Effects of the Sanctions on Russia', *The World Economy*, 2025.

Sanctions, countersanctions and secondary sanctions (and their linked threats) are now an integral part of international economic reality, akin to other policies with pervasive cross-border and intertemporal effects; therefore, they deserve to be analysed in an unbiased and fully transparent manner, rather than skirted.

The nomenclature of war is routinely teleported by researchers, albeit selectively, perhaps in a nod to being sensitive and to avoid controversy. A sanctioned country, the recipient, is called 'target'; the book uses these two words interchangeably. A sanctioning authority[9] is termed 'sender'—a polite term as in 'sending a vacation postcard from distant lands'; 'targeter' would perhaps be more apt and help make the war analogy complete.

Sanctions have been described as 'siege warfare' and their ends are to be achieved by 'weakening the enemy'. Academic articles on economic sanctions revel in using 'new weapons', 'weaponised tariffs', 'the weapons race', 'precision-guided economic munitions' etc. Even the term 'smart weapons'

---

9 Can be a country, a grouping of countries or a multilateral body (usually the United Nations).

has been usurped into 'smart[10] (or targeted) sanctions'; and the dictum that truth is the first casualty of war is equally true of sanctions ('smart sanctions are not harmful to anyone else!'). Smart, as opposed to comprehensive, sanctions have coincided with an *unending proliferation of secondary sanctions*, indirectly implying that for the former to work, the latter *force-multiplier* is necessary (see **Figure 1.1**).[11] Secondary sanctions are to primary sanctions what drones are to ballistic missiles.

---

10 These are known as *list-based* sanctions, which have 'allowed the US government to more precisely target persons and groups who pose a threat to national security, foreign policy, and economy of the United States; list-based sanctions have been particularly helpful from a law enforcement perspective of the US Treasury's Office of Foreign Assets Control.' The 9/11 attacks in 2001 are cited as catalyst for US smart sanctions ('to minimize the suffering of innocent civilians'). The President's Executive Order 13224 on 23 September 2001 provided US Treasury Department officials with 'far reaching authority to freeze the assets and financial transactions of individuals and other entities suspected of supporting terrorism'. In conjunction with the USA Patriot Act, 'Treasury [Department] needs only a *reasonable suspicion* (my emphasis)—not necessarily *any* evidence—to target entities under these laws'. (Masters, Jonathan, 'What Are Economic Sanctions?', Council on Foreign Relations, 2024).

11 Smart sanctions are obviously not so smart: given macroeconomic interlinkages and the dominance of the US dollar in global liquidity provision, cutting off payments' mechanisms for, say, specific transactions have unforeseen collateral consequences. Smart sanctions engender multiple externalities.

Figure 1.1: High Frequency Snapshot of Secondary Sanctions*

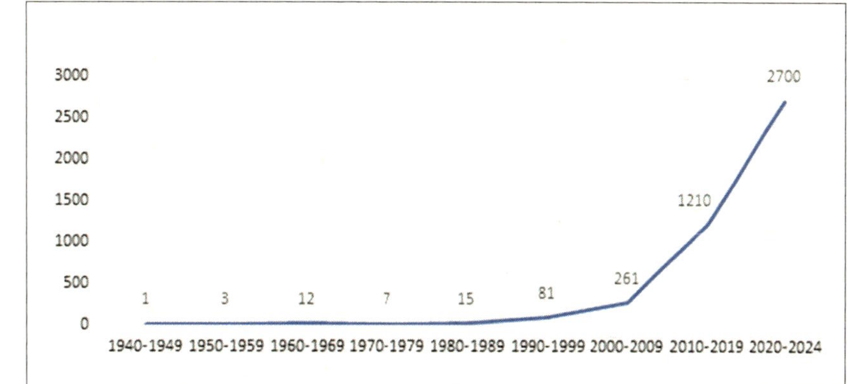

*The number of results returned for 'secondary sanctions'.

Source: Google Scholar, accessed on 16 November 2024.

Hardly a month passes without reports of further sanctions, usually secondary ones, oftentimes under the radar; the *sui generis* 'whack-a-mole' nature of these measures adds to their capriciousness, on par with a turn of the roulette wheel. Sanctions are a persistent headwind for the global economy—one that does not subside, only arbitrarily strengthens over time. The *network* effects of such unidirectional expansion—*sanctions deepening,*[12] if you will—cannot be negligible.

Updating the Lexicon

Another evocative analogy harks back to cowboy movies, where the country imposing sanctions gathers a 'posse' of like-minded allies—the good guys to punish the bad guy, the target.

The extant nomenclature is utterly reflective of a sanctioner's mindset that, inevitably, carries bias. It is natural, therefore, that the lexicon is expanded to bring it up to date in consonance with the war-like attributes of current usage, and the sensibilities of sanctioned countries and third parties.

1. The sanctioning entity should be labelled the (primary) *sanctioner* or targeter.
2. Secondary sanctions and the accompanying *ricochet* should be a central part of the discussion, as they affect an expanding list of countries and sectors—the *secondary sanctioned.* These extraterritorial

12 Pernicious analogue of capital deepening.

sanctions are enforced to impede the economic and commercial activity of governments and businesses of third countries; they are a means of influencing the decisions of countries that would not otherwise be in violation of a sanctioner's primary sanctions.[13] Consequences—instantaneous, lagged and *long-lasting*—are felt in the balance of payments, domestic investment, creditworthiness of projects and the government's fiscal position. This is an *economic externality* on which little quantitative light has been shed.

---

13 Primary sanctions apply to the sanctioning country's persons or to instances where there is a sanctioning country involvement; it covers contribution of a sanctioning-country person, and sanctioning-country goods or transactions that take place within the sanctioning country's borders vis-a vis the target country. Secondary sanctions are imposed to prevent third parties/victims (not subject to the sanctioner's legal jurisdiction) from dealing with a target (and entities therein) that is subject to sanctions issued by a (primary) sanctioner, even if these third parties are not citizens of the sanctioning country or based in the sanctioning country; they face penalties for doing business with the targeted country or individuals. About secondary sanctions, the US, which is by far the dominant sanctioner, authorises the Office of Foreign Assets Control or the State Department to threaten sanctions on a person, including a non-US citizen, for a specified activity. The sanctions are intended to discourage non-US persons from participating in specific transactions, even if these transactions are not subject to primary sanctions. Distinct from primary sanctions that are enforced by fines or seizure of US-held assets, the secondary sanctions instrumentality is heavily dependent on the importance of the US financial system and the use of the US dollar as the global numeraire (unit of account) and the principal currency for settling cross-border transactions.

For India, the list of 'designations and updates' has 85 entries (related to Russia, Iran, Syria, Cuba, North Korea, anti-/counter-terrorism and arms proliferation) on the US Office of Foreign Assets Control (OFAC) website.[14] Brazil has 39 entries and China has 284.[15] Traversing the intricacies of a sanctions regime—with the danger of being summarily debarred from activities on *suspicion* of transgression—can be tricky and increases the cost of doing business.

For a condensed illustration of complications for India, see **Table 1.2** for a sectoral breakdown and **Table 1.3** for the country of origin of the entities in India that have violated US sanctions.

14 Financial sector compliance has been the most responsive area. Indian banks have generally been careful about transactions that could trigger secondary sanctions, often over-complying to avoid US financial system access issues. This has created real constraints on certain international business activities.

15 A search on the OFAC website for secondary sanctions throws up 3,990 results of which 674 are Russia-related (as of July 2025).

Table 1.2: India: Impacted Sectors

Sector	Number of entities
Agriculture	1
Electronics Components (semiconductor distribution)	1
Financial	4
Food and Beverage	2
Information Technology	1
Petrochemical	3
Petroleum and Petroleum Products	1
LNG Tanker	1
Sea and Coastal Freight	1
Shipping and Maritime	9
Technology and Digital Transformation	1
Telecommunications	1
Tobacco Products	1
Transportation	1
Travel and Hospitality	1

Table 1.3: India: Countries of Origin

Country of origin	Number of entities
China	1
Hong Kong	1
India	16
Iran	1
N. Korea	1
Russia	4
UAE	5

Source for Tables 1.2 and 1.3: United States, Department of the Treasury, Office of Foreign Assets Control (OFAC), *Sanctions Programs and Information*. Data compiled November 2024.

3. Third parties can legitimately be identified as *victims* of the collateral damage schemed by sanctions and secondary sanctions.
4. The US is the hegemonic sanctioner.[16] (Caution and apology: This may strike as biased; however, given the undoubted pre-eminence, by a considerable distance, of the US government as policy practitioner around sanctions, it cannot be helped.) The EU tends to coordinate with the US on some sanctions but maintains its own legal framework and decision-making process, often resulting in fewer and less comprehensive sanctions compared to the US approach (see **Appendix 1**).
5. Sanctions busters christened, disparagingly, 'black knight states' are *white knights* for sanctioned countries and resultant victims.
6. China, Eurasia and the transitivity of geography spawned by physical proximity are significant elements. Accept China as a practical 'safe harbour'—a *hegemon saviour* of sorts—more so for countries caught up in the vortex of sanctions in Asia and the neighbourhood.[17]

---

16 It is analogous to labelling the US as an economic hegemon—an expression that is widely used.

17 China provides various forms of assistance to sanctioned countries, often through mechanisms that attempt to navigate or circumvent Western sanctions while maintaining plausible deniability. It engages in extensive barter trade and commodity swaps, exchanging manufactured goods for oil, gas or raw materials without traditional currency transactions; this has been particularly evident with Iran and Russia.

7. We should situate the relatively unfamiliar international financial architecture that is gradually shaping up around the New Development Bank (NDB), sponsored by Brazil, Russia, India, China and South Africa (the BRICS countries), and the AIIB, where China, India and Russia are the largest shareholders) as a risk mitigant; a rational response to the ever-expanding sanctions blanket.

Tweak the Approach

The book, *inter alia*, attempts to make a case for the following adjustments:

(i) Re-examine and augment the definition of payoff to the sanctioner(s). Pay attention to externalities for a fuller comprehension of the ramifications of sanctions and secondary sanctions. At present, the incidence of *harm* to third countries is underappreciated (behind a veil).

(ii) Modulate the classification of a successful sanctions regime. We have to diverge from the binary/discrete 'success' or 'failure' barometer to make sense of orthodox observations. Specifically, rationalise the yardstick of evaluation by *granularising* it.

(iii) It is not unreasonable that an emerging market perspective is necessary.

(iv) We must include accretion of sanctions and secondary sanctions, and the externality inherent in them as a *source* of policy-induced (global) economic uncertainty, similar (at par) to (with) the destabilising global macro shocks emanating from (occasionally erratic) announcements and implementation of conventional macroeconomic policies—monetary and fiscal—of systemic economies, viz., the US, the EU and China. The doubt and fear engendered by the frequency of fresh sanctions is non-trivial,[18] with its inbuilt 'extra turn of the screw' bias. There is rationale for a sanctions calculator; policy estimates of externalities can provide, *inter alia*, navigational beacons for the possibility, however remote, of course correction or an off-ramp.

Uncertainty and trepidation around secondary sanctions is not theoretical; anticipation effects on investment are real. Ponder over the following timeline of development of Iran's Chabahar Port with Indian investment:

- Talks started in 2003; subsequently, US sanctions targeting Iran put a hard break.
- Talks revived after the US eased sanctions in 2015 under the Iran nuclear deal.
- Tripartite agreement signed by Iran, Afghanistan and India in 2016.
- In 2017, the first shipment of Indian wheat to

18 I can personally vouch from direct professional experience that the unpredictability and threat of secondary sanctions, especially through the external payments channel, has created a miasma for third countries on the real likelihood of discrimination and disproportionate punishment that is embedded in them.

Afghanistan was unloaded at Chabahar.

- In 2018, the US withdrew from the nuclear deal, and 'reintroduced maximum pressure sanctions' on Iran. This limited operations at Chabahar Port.
- In 2024, after India had signed a 10-year agreement with Iran to develop and operate Chabahar Port, the US State Department at a press briefing in May said: 'Any entity, anyone considering business deals with Iran, they need to be aware of the potential risk that they are opening themselves up to and the potential risk of sanctions.'[19] India has been warned! (See **Appendix 2** for a back-of-the-envelope estimate of the financial cost of the start-stop project.)

(v) Address the scantiness of information on who bears the cost of sanctions. It is critical to *disentangle* the effects on the global economy of continuing wars, sanctions, and the mushrooming of secondary sanctions on third countries. The international media disregards this facet *in toto*. For example, can anyone recall when was the last time an analyst based in a sanctions-impacted country was interviewed by the BBC or CNN? It is noteworthy that, on the eve of the 16th Annual BRICS Summit in Kazan, Russia on 22 October 2024, the BBC's designated expert analyst on the topic was an academic based in Ireland.

---

19 Lawal, Shola, 'Does India Risk US Sanctions Over Iran's Chabahar Port Deal?', *Al Jazeera*, 17 May 2024, https://tinyurl.com/2ta2zs43. Accessed on 8 September 2025.

The plan for the rest of the book is as follows:

In **Chapter 2**, incongruity in aspects of the sanctions discourse is identified, and explanations are offered to square the circle.

The next two chapters present indicative formal templates; they try to shed light on interesting analytical dimensions based on convenient assumptions, rather than representing fully worked-out academically rigorous models. A systems approach to sanctions and countermeasures that expounds leakage, lags, policy gyrations and hysteresis is presented in **Chapter 3**; rough and ready applications to granular data from Iran and Belarus is attempted. **Chapter 4** delineates, through an illustrative example, the conditions that determine effectiveness of *more* sanctions and secondary sanctions to give a sense on the importance of *cross-marginal* impacts—that determine *strategic impeders* and *strategic reinforcers*—for overall payoff of the targeter.

In **Chapter 5**, *choices* of important stakeholders, specifically multilateral institutions—G20, IMF and World Bank—to eschew transparency on the welfare repercussions of sanctions, secondary sanctions, countersanctions and the externalities innate in these policies is highlighted.

Chapter 6 discusses the meta themes on Renminbi internationalisation against the backdrop of China as a 'white knight'—a saviour for economies mainly sanctioned by the West. There are gaps, identified by an unconventional, but not misplaced, lens in the 'operating system' that have occluded China's currency project.

Concluding remarks are offered in **Chapter 7**.

2

DISSONANCE, AND SUGGESTIONS FOR SQUARING THE CIRCLE

Dissonance #1: Number of sanctions and (perceived) ineffectiveness

ON BALANCE, FORMAL academic data suggest that economic sanctions are not that successful in effectuating stated objective(s) of the sanctioner (See **Figure 2.1** for a high-frequency picture.)

Out of 909 sanctions since 2000, less than one-fifth are judged 'total successes'; when 'partially successful', which number 62, are added to the count of 'total success', the fraction is one-fourth (GSDB-R4).[1;2] It can be argued that recent sanctions have not had sufficient time to gain traction and reach thresholds that force targets to change behaviour.

Figure 2.1: High Frequency Snapshot of Sanctions*

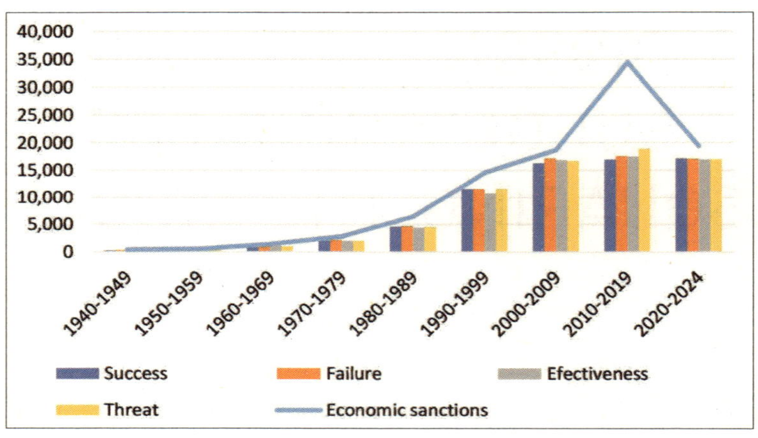

*The number of results returned for 'economic sanctions', 'success', 'failure', 'effectiveness' and 'threat'.
Source: *Google Scholar*, accessed on 16 November 2024.

There are many sanctions that do not end—close to watching paint drying. Reflect on two examples, viz., sanctions on Nigeria by the US in 2003 are ongoing; those by the EU on Moldova in 2003 are continuing. These are either where there is a failure to recognise that they have been futile, or, there is expectation of success, or, perhaps

1 Global Sanctions Data Base (GSDB-R4), LeBow College of Business, Drexel University, 2025.

2 There are 18 instances of 'negotiated settlement'.

forgotten by sanctioning bureaucracies! There are instances when recognition of miscalculation was swift—sanctions on India in 1998 were lifted within 2–3 years of imposition. Others, like that on Uzbekistan during 2003–2012 by the US failed after being active for a decade. Heterogeneity in behaviour of a sanctioner along the dimension of length of sanctions on a target necessitates reasoning; later in the chapter a framework is sketched to elucidate this.

Unsurprisingly, the US stands out as a sanctioner:[3] of the 1,547 sanctions since 1949 globally, 589 have been *by* (and/or involve) the US, and 12 have been *on* the US (most recently countersanctions by China, Russia and Iran for obvious reasons).[4] US-led sanctions jumped in recent decades, supposedly due to the collapse of the Soviet Union (see **Table 2.1**).[5] OFAC administers around three dozen sanctions programmes. It is noteworthy that the fraction of sanctions on Asian countries by other Asian countries has come down after the height of the Cold War in the 1970s (see **Table 2.2**).

---

3 The US imposed *comprehensive* curbs on Cuba (since 1960), North Korea (2006), Iran (1979), Russia (2014) and Syria (2004, after being designated as a sponsor of terrorism in 1979). The US currently administers 37 sanctions programmes, one of which pertains to 'Chinese Military Companies' (*United States Department of the Treasury, Office of Foreign Assets Control (OFAC)*, https://ofac.treasury.gov/. Accessed in July 2025).

4 Total active sanctions by the US are reported to be more than 15,000; presumably this is inclusive of secondary sanctions at the individuals' and entities' levels (Stein, Jeff, and Federica Cocco, 'How Four US Presidents Unleashed Economic Warfare Across the Globe', *The Washington Post*, 25 July 2024. https://tinyurl.com/yf69awht. Accessed on 9 September 2025).

5 The second largest non-UN sanctioner after the US is the EU.

Table 2.1: Number of Sanctions by Major Sanctioners/Targeters

Country/Grouping	1990–2023	2000–2023
US	442	365
EU	159	122

Table 2.2: Sanctions on Asia* (noticeable step up after the 1980s)

Decade	Number of fresh sanctions	of which by Asia on Asia (per cent)
1950s	17	3 (17)
1960s	23	9 (39)
1970s	27	8 (30)
1980s	25	2 (8)
1990s	56	4 (7)
2000s	53	8 (15)
2010–2023	102**	13 (13)

*Excluding Russia; includes Central Asia.

**Main targets: North Korea (18), Myanmar (17), China (17), Afghanistan (11), Cambodia (11), Indonesia (7), Taiwan (6), Pakistan (4), Philippines (4).

Source for Tables 2.1 and 2.2: GSDB-R4, 2025;[6] Felbermayr et al., 2020;[7] Yalcin et al., 2025[8]

---

6 Global Sanctions Data Base (GSDB-R4), LeBow College of Business, Drexel University, 2025.

7 Felbermayr, Gabriel J., Aleksandra Kirilakha, Constantinos Syropoulos, Erdal Yalcin, and Yoto V. Yotov, 'The Global Sanctions Data Base', *European Economic Review,* vol. 129, 2020, pp. 1–23.

8 Yalcin, Erdal, Gabriel Felbermayr, Heider Kariem, Aleksandra Kirilakha, Ohyun Kwon, Constantinos Syropoulos, and Yoto V. Yotov, 'The Global Sanctions Data Base—Release 4: The Heterogeneous Effects of the Sanctions on Russia', *The World Economy*, 2025.

Much of the empirical work on determining the economic effects of smart sanctions centres on a target country around trade in goods and services that are adjacent to this exchange (for recent examples see Ahn and Ludema, 2020[9] and Egger et al., 2024).[10] The spectrum of economic sanctions has ballooned from trade curbs, military embargoes and end-use restrictions on bilateral foreign aid to a macro-financial inventory compounded by elaborate secondary sanctions—a fluid catalogue of 'do nots' on third parties—comprising banking, capital markets, insurance, pressure on multilateral development banks and limiting (official) debt-servicing capacity, which have a bearing on credit rating and solvency (see **Table 2.3**).[11]

9 Ahn, Daniel P., and Rodney D. Ludema, 'The Sword and the Shield: The Economics of Targeted Sanctions', *European Economic Review*, vol. 130, 2020, 103587.

10 Egger, Peter, Constantinos Syropoulos, and Yoto V. Yotov, 'Analysing the Effects of Economic Sanctions: Recent Theory, Data, and Quantification', *Review of International Economics*, vol. 32, 2024, pp. 1–11.

11 A report from the World Economic Forum in 2025 finds: 'Financial system fragmentation can have a negative impact by decreasing global economic output and increasing inflation. This report presents new analysis indicating that one-year economic output losses from fragmentation could range from [US]$0.6 trillion to [US]$5.7 trillion, or about 5 percent of current global gross domestic product (GDP) and twice the output losses caused by the COVID-19 pandemic, depending on the degree of fragmentation. Similarly, inflation rises steadily in most countries as fragmentation increases, which is likely to necessitate higher interest rates and have an impact on borrowing costs for individuals, businesses and governments.' ('Navigating Global Financial System Fragmentation', *World Economic Forum*, January, 2025).

Table 2.3: Evolution of Sanctions by Type

Decade	Trade	Financial	Travel	Military Assistance	Arms
1950s	27	14	8	1	7
1960s	30	29	8	13	29
1970s	47	54	4	23	11
1980s	52	51	21	13	19
1990s	77	148	32	58	69
2000s	71	103	68	71	63
2010–2023	283	483	281	72	82

Source: GSDB-R4, 2025;[12] Felbermayr et al, 2020;[13] Yalcin et al., 2025[14]

12 Global Sanctions Data Base (GSDB-R4), LeBow College of Business, Drexel University, 2025.

13 Felbermayr, Gabriel J., Aleksandra Kirilakha, Constantinos Syropoulos, Erdal Yalcin, and Yoto V. Yotov, 'The Global Sanctions Data Base', *European Economic Review*, vol. 129, 2020, pp. 1–23.

14 Yalcin, Erdal, Gabriel Felbermayr, Heider Kariem, Aleksandra Kirilakha, Ohyun Kwon, Constantinos Syropoulos, and Yoto V. Yotov, 'The Global Sanctions Data Base—Release 4: The Heterogeneous Effects of the Sanctions on Russia', *The World Economy*, 2025.

The low success rate of sanctions over the decades is striking, according to surveys by long-standing researchers: Hufbauer and J.J. Schott (1985)[15] and Hufbauer et al. (2007)[16]: 34 per cent; Pape (1997)[17]: 5 per cent; Smeets (2018)[18] and van Bergeijk (2021).[19] Kirilakha et al. (2021)[20] find that the average success rate of sanctions is 40 per cent. When threats are added to the mix the following conclusion is sobering: 'However, a remarkable observation about economic sanctions is that they often fail to generate significant costs. According to the Threat and Imposition of Sanctions (TIES) dataset, 82 per cent of imposed sanctions between 1945 and 2005 produced only minor costs to the target state.'[21] (See **Figure 2.2**).

---

15 Hufbauer, Gary C. and Jeffrey J. Schott, *Economic Sanctions Reconsidered: History and Current Policy*, Peterson Institute for International Economics, Washington D.C., 1985.

16 Hufbauer, Gary C., Jeffrey J. Schott, Kimberley Ann Elliott, and Barbara Oegg, *Economic Sanctions Reconsidered*, 3rd ed., Peterson Institute for International Economics, Washington D.C., 2007.

17 Pape, Robert A., 'Why Economic Sanctions Do Not Work', *International Security*, vol. 22, 1997, pp. 90–136.

18 Smeets, Maarten, 'Can Economic Sanctions Be Effective', *ERSD Staff Working Paper Series*, World Trade Organization, Geneva, 2018.

19 van Bergeijk, Peter A.G., ed., *The Research Handbook on Economic Sanctions*, Elgaronline, Northampton, MA, 2021.

20 Kirilakha, Aleksandra, Gabriel J. Felbermayr, Constantinos Syropoulos, Erdal Yalcin, and Yoto V. Yotov, 'The Global Sanctions Data Base: An Update That Includes the Years of the Trump Presidency', *The Research Handbook on Economic Sanctions*, Peter A.G. van Bergeijk (ed.), Elgaronline, 2021, pp. 62–106.

21 Cilizoglu, Menevis, and Navin Bapat, 'Economic Coercion and the Problem of Sanctions-Proofing', *Conflict Management and Peace Science*, vol. 37, 2020, pp. 385–408.

Figure 2.2: Are Threats Ineffective?

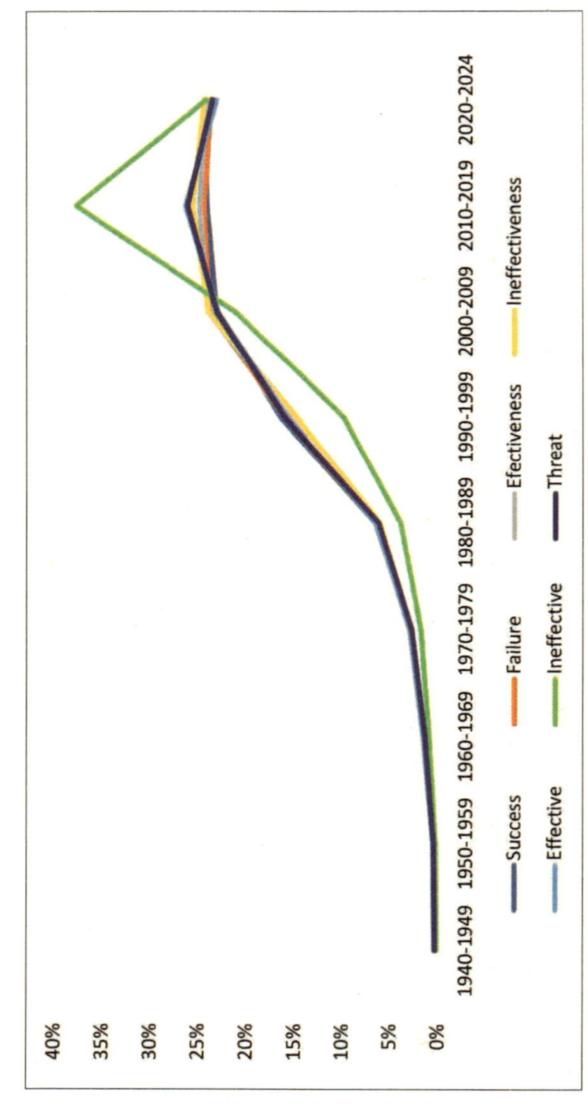

Source: *Google Scholar*, accessed on 16 November 2024.

There are researchers who argue that sanctions effectiveness cannot be reliably gauged quantitatively, by applying statistical/econometric criteria, because of disagreement/confusion/subjectivity over valid metrics (Pala, 2021;[22] Peksen, 2019[23]).[24] Alternatively, there are hidden abstract interests of targeters that are unobservable.

On the face of it, if something is not working there should be less of it, not more. And yet there is no drop in the number of new sanctions: in the 1990s the number of sanctions were 270; 2000–2009: 213; and 2010–2023: 696.

To the numbers in the previous paragraphs, the long (and lengthening) shadow of secondary sanctions (along with other strictures), which are a multiple of primary sanctions, must be *conjoined.* Secondary sanctions have first-order effects on victims as these force third countries to deviate from optimal commercial preferences. The US has pioneered secondary sanctions on an industrial scale, with cooperative and synchronised overlapping by its posse, the G7/EU. The handbrake has been taken off for imposing sanctions; there are virtually no guardrails. (It is reported that the US was responsible for 'three times as many sanctions as any other

22 Pala, Tadeas, 'The Effectiveness of Economic Sanctions: A Literature Review', *The NISPACEE Journal of Public Administration and Policy*, vol. XIV, Summer 2021, pp. 239–259.

23 Peksen, Dursun, 'When Do Imposed Economic Sanctions Work? A Critical Review of the Sanctions Effectiveness Literature', *Defence and Peace Economics*, vol. 30, 2019, pp. 635–647.

24 A failure by researchers to not distinguish between 'effectiveness' and 'efficiency' of sanctions is put forward as one of the underpinnings of the confusion.

country or international body...')[25] The only constraint on maximising economic harm on a target is the self-harm to the sanctioner.

Secondary sanction circumscriptions are unsettled—a moving target—and open to interpretation, which can be inordinately lengthy, resultantly damaging as *risk aversion* compels a standstill on commercial decisions; this is a driver for enormous uncertainty—more than a dysfunctional WTO has—for wide-ranging categories of international commerce, and poses an anticipatory *hazard* for literally dozens of jurisdictions around the world. Is there a method to the chaos? While there are questions around the success of sanctions, there is clarity on why sanctions are forced: catalyse change in a target's policies that are detrimental to the sanctioner, leaving aside oft-cited highfalutin bromide such as enforcing 'international norms of behaviour'. A target's policies should be congruent with the sanctioner's requirement, or, else!

Dissonance #2

Despite empirically persuasive that sanctions are ineffective, few scholars *conclude* that sanctioners should eschew this policy. Instead, proposals for making sanctions more effective (smarter!) and diminishing sanctions-proofing are

---

25 '...targeting a *third* (my emphasis) of all nations with some kind of financial penalty on people, properties or organizations.' (Stein, Jeff, and Federica Cocco, 'How Four US Presidents Unleashed Economic Warfare Across the Globe', *The Washington Post*, 25 July 2024. https://tinyurl.com/yf69awht. Accessed on 9 September 2025).

the order of the day. It is in the professional wellbeing of the ecosystem around sanctions in the US and the EU to convince policymakers that it is viable to *seek a silk purse out of a sow's ear.*[26]

Is the quest for more effective sanctions instruments a fool's errand lubricated by directly unproductive profit-seeking (DUP) economic activity reminiscent of lobbying for rents around discretionary trade protectionism and government interventions more generally?[27]

If the current sanctions regimes resemble Swiss cheese with a limited chance of pushing the target to its knees, it behoves stakeholders, led by independent researchers and analysts—soothsayers of our times—based in sanctioning countries, to call this out, instead of self-indulgent ventriloquising apropos making sanctions more effective inasmuch as 'great powers' can do this.[28] An expression that comes to mind is: *honey badger don't care.*

---

26 An idiom: 'To produce something refined, admirable, or valuable from something which is unrefined, unpleasant, or of little or no value.'

27 See: Krueger, Anne, 'The Political Economy of the Rent-Seeking Society', American Economic Review, vol. 64, 1974, pp. 291–303; and Bhagwati, Jagdish, and T.N. Srinivasan, 'The Welfare Consequences of Directly-Unproductive Profit-Seeking (DUP) Lobbying Activities: Price versus Quantity Distortions', *Journal of International Economics*, vol. 13, 1978, pp. 33–44.

28 Early, Bryan R., 'Making Sanctions Work: Promoting Compliance, Punishing Violations, and Discouraging Sanctions Busting', *The Research Handbook on Economic Sanctions*, Peter A.G. van Bergeijk (ed.), Elgaronline, 2021.

Dissonance #3

Whereas wars and foreign policy are matters of electoral politics, economic sanctions are rarely debated. Why? A reasonable hypothesis is that there is not enough firm and coherent numbers to inform the debate. In contrast, calculations of impact on consumer prices of standard trade barriers (for example, tariffs on washing machines) are available, but barely anything concrete on effects of sanctions on the pocketbook of the average citizen. Politicians rarely take credit for them and voters neither ask questions nor blame elected officials for their ineffectiveness. Voters come to know the tangible cost of wars, both human lives and spent treasure; on the other hand, cost-benefit of sanctions, countersanctions and secondary sanctions are a black box—the layered and complex scope is a mystery to most[29] (smog #1).

A US dollar estimate of the costs has the potential to inform citizens in whose name sanctions are applied by sanctioning governments; absent solid numbers, the subject matter is, well, too esoteric for public policy scrutiny. There is the odd exception when politicians are acutely aware of a domestic ideological by-product, such as imposing or lifting end-use limitations on foreign humanitarian aid for family planning arising out of voter preference.[30]

---

29 The bulk of smart sanctions are 'unknown to the general public' (Hufbauer, Gary C., and Eujin Jung, 'What's New in Economic Sanctions?', *European Economic Review*, vol. 130, 2020, pp. 1–12.).

30 There is a clockwork five-year cycle in the US on the policy of US funding for nongovernmental organizations that offer abortion-related services abroad. First enacted in 1985, depending on which of the two

Rationalisation

Squaring the Circle

The above paragraphs have an undercurrent of irrational behaviour of sanctioners—they hanker for more sanctions just as they are reckoned to be ineffective, and voters appear detached.

A presupposition for the incongruence could be that the sanctions technology is becoming less effective; hence more sanctions, both primary and secondary, are needed to attain effectiveness.

It is maintainable that not enough time has elapsed for recent sanctions to bite the target adequately. (After all, even military wars must cross (minimal) boundaries of physical damage to the target to elicit change in behaviour.) An example could be that exhausting the target's foreign exchange reserves is time-consuming with long lags.

Is this due to the rise of China in the last fifteen years and its emergence as a hegemon saviour? Owing to its economic prowess, complemented by its location straddling eastern and central Asia, China is better positioned to assist countries (partially) neutralise Western-led sanctions than the erstwhile Soviet Union ever was during its halcyon days as a military superpower, but short of economic and financial heft.

---

main parties is in the majority in the legislature, the so-called Mexico City Policy has been enforced only under Republican governments and rolled back when the Democratic Party wins the White House (Moss, Kellie, Jennifer Kates, Anna Rouw, and Stephanie Oum, 'What the Election Could Mean for the Mexico City Policy and US Foreign Aid', *Global Health Policy*, 2024.).

How does one explain these representative conformities?

Explanation #1

Augment the payoff accounting:

We can explicitly bring into the cost–benefit calculation the externalities and shadow benefits from the sanctioner's vantage point; if these are *internalised*, then perhaps the increase in sanctions by an optimising sanctioner is justified.

At the outset, it is logical to assume that sanctions and secondary sanctions are designed to cause economic harm to other countries, *contingent* on the constraint of acceptable cost borne by the sanctioner.

Let us briefly explore a constitutive breakdown:

B is the positive payoff to the sanctioner. It has two direct components: (i) harm to the target (which is the proximate motive for imposing sanctions and secondary sanctions); and, (ii) direct benefit to the sanctioner by expanding its market footprint (for example, increased oil and natural gas exports by the US to the EU substituted Russian energy in the global market).

D comprises direct cost (bureaucracy, information dissemination, economic aid as a sweetener to allies, harnessing diplomatic capital to convince partners, etc.) incurred by the sanctioner plus *self-harm*—a cost (negative payoff) for a sanctioner and its partners (spillback), incorporating blowback from countersanctions by the target. For instance, foregoing essential imports required by the sanctioner and loss of business. Self-harm/cost to the sanctioner increasingly includes (gradual) currency substitution away from the international numeraire; an adverse reputation effect due to violation of the payments facilitating obligation (reliability discount).[31]

E is a positive *non-pecuniary* externality that benefits the sanctioner's calculation in two ways: (i) countries on whom secondary sanctions are thrust induce them to lean on the target to listen to the sanctioner, so it is advantageous for the latter to magnify the negative externality on the third party/innocent bystander (*indirect complementarity*); and (ii) a pre-emptive coercion/demonstration effect, a form of *signal* to potentially unobliging adversaries; it is (symbolically) useful as it burnishes the tough guy image of the sanctioner when differences of opinion arise in the future. To put it simply, *fear has value.*

S represents the second externality: harmful *pecuniary* spillovers on non-allies of sanctions on the target and (threat) of secondary sanctions on third countries (present and future); these are, not uncommonly, emerging economies. (The secondary tariffs of 25 per cent by the US, in August 2025, on Indian exports as reprisal for buying Russian oil would fall in this 'bucket'.) This is an economic loss (tangible collateral damage) that the sanctioner should weigh up but likely does not.

The observed/naïve payoff that the sanctioner seemingly maximises is B – D. The effective one for the sanctioner is B – D + E. The complete payoff for the sanctioner should be B – D + E – S. It is in the sanctioner's interest to internalise

---

31 Further, a sense of alienation by third parties towards the sanctioner increases.

(the unobservable) E and ignore S; its demand for sanctions is higher than merely optimising over B – D. Researchers may not be giving the requisite weight to E while they bemoan that the larger number of sanctions by sanctioners in recent decades have not been commensurately successful. From the sanctioner's standpoint, underplaying S, or applying only a small weight, helps to preserve the overall attractiveness of its sanctions policy. More generally, a sanctioner can, of course, choose to apply specific weights on each of the components B, D, E and S.

The upshot is that the sanctioner's effective *marginal benefit curve* for sanctions is to the right of the notional demand one if we plot effectiveness of sanctions minus cost (y-axis) against quantum of sanctions (x-axis) (see **Figure 2.3**).

Figure 2.3: Marginal Benefit Curve of the Sanctioner

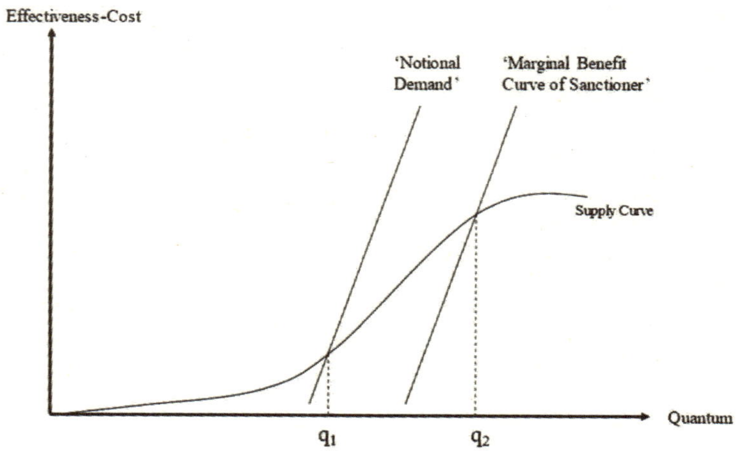

Supply of sanctions is determined by the sanctions technology. It is less effective by 'leakage' (courtesy white knights) and normal trade substitution. But more effective if direct economic harm to target through increment of an extensive array of instruments is drawn upon to, *inter alia*, drain away confidence from target's economy, viz. withdrawal of hard currency liquidity, downward impact on equity market valuation owing to announcement effects on international portfolio reallocations, nudge a credit rating downgrade, external commercial borrowing hindrances, etc. A pivot of the *effective sanctions supply curve* is feasible.

Has sanctions technology, at the margin, become less effective?

Overusing the US dollar correspondent banking node as a 'switch' on payments (on target and secondary sanctioned entities) has instigated many countries to *counter-programme* by exploring alternatives over the last decade or so, which inevitably undercuts the US dollar's paramount currency status.

Discretionary *legal loophole/leakage*—akin to triple flip backs—in the sanctions and secondary sanctions architecture are a prerogative of a powerful sanctioner to mitigate self-harm for itself and its kindred pack. There are two recent examples:

- Russian oil exports of several million barrels per day are allowed to ensure that the global market-clearing oil price is within *politically* tolerable limits of the US and the EU, seeing domestic inflation in the West is a hot-button electoral issue. Much as the EU depicts

China and India as sanctions-busters, the EU relies on third-country refiners that legally buy Russian oil to meet its demand for refined products; international financial payment sanctions for Russia have been kept ajar for this.[32] India and China are the white knights for softening the unfavourable terms-of-trade (TOT) effect that would come about with certainty if Russian oil did not reach global markets.

- Russia's exports of enriched uranium have not been appreciably curbed as it is the world's largest supplier. Many NATO-affiliated countries depend on Russia for more than half of their enriched uranium, and about a quarter of the commodity used by US nuclear power plants is from Russia.

In contrast, it has been reported that unpaid dividend income of India's public sector oil companies from their Russian upstream 'oil equity' investments, made over the years, has accumulated to around US$900 million.[33] This is a result of payment channel-related prohibitions by the US and the EU. Non-receipt of this income, *inter alia*, affects

---

32 Russian sanctions have shown India's limits in compliance. India has continued purchasing Russian oil at increased volumes through 2024, often using alternative payment mechanisms to avoid direct US financial system exposure. Indian companies have been more cautious about defence cooperation and technology transfers, but haven't fundamentally altered the relationship.

33 See, for example, Sharma, Sukalp, 'Indian Oil PSUs' Dividends Stuck in Russia Swell to Around $900 Million as Repatriation Efforts Flounder', *The Indian Express*, 19 September 2024, https://tinyurl.com/3nc4v6wk. Accessed on 9 September 2025.

investments by Indian oil companies and the government's budgetary revenue.

Russia has a 30 per cent share in the production of rough diamonds, and India cuts 14 out of 15 of the world's rough diamonds. Diamonds of carat size 0.5 and above that are imported by India from Russia[34] for cutting and polishing cannot be sold in the G7 and EU.

In August 2025 the US imposed, for perhaps the first time ever, (generalised) secondary tariffs for indirect economic ties.[35] Over one-half of India's merchandise exports to the US now attracts an *additional* 25 per cent tariff as punishment for India's legal oil imports (and implicitly purchase of military hardware) from Russia. The stated objective is to reduce Russia's oil receipts (from one country), and thereby its capacity to fight the war in Ukraine. Other large importers of Russian energy—China, Turkey and the EU, amongst others—have been spared; China because of its leverage of the rare earths' ecosystem (raw material and manufacture of magnets); Turkey and the EU for, presumably, the overlap with NATO membership.[36]

The US policy change represents a dramatic departure from

---

34 Third country workarounds have been reported (Ghosal, Sugata Ghosh and Sutanuka, 'Indian Businesses Take UAE Route for Russian Payments', *The Economic Times*, 13 May 2022, https://tinyurl.com/yt7bjbh8. Accessed on 9 September 2025.).

35 In March 2025 an executive order authorised secondary tariffs of 25 per cent on countries that import Venezuelan oil; no country has been designated under that order.

36 Russia's top five pipeline gas consumers are Germany, Italy, Belarus, Turkey and the Netherlands. The top five LNG consumers of Russian gas are Japan, China, France, Spain and Taiwan.

the previous rule on Russian oil exports. Since late 2022, the US had backed the G7 Russia Oil Price Cap plan, which permitted Russia to continue selling oil while using sanctions to keep prices artificially low. The EU, in July 2025, announced a reduction in the price ceiling, effective September, from US$60 to US$47.60 per barrel, but the US did not sign up for this constricted cap. It remains to be seen whether the EU will take steps to shadow the US policy on India.

A secondary tariff on a wide swathe of an exporter's economy is, without exaggeration, the 'big daddy' in the secondary sanctions' armoury. The direct economic blow to India of the August secondary sanctions—early estimates vary from 0.2 per cent to 0.8 per cent of GDP—is *prima facie* larger than that of sanctions imposed on India in previous decades (see **Appendix 3** for a description of past major episodes of sanctions).[37] Depending on the duration of the secondary tariffs, the cumulative welfare loss for India is

---

37 India has been a sanctioner since independence; Pakistan was successfully sanctioned over the period 1949–51 for territorial matters. India imposed sanctions on Portugal from 1954–61 over the status of Goa, which was eventually liberated by India in 1961. Since 1989, Nepal has been sanctioned thrice, with the latest episode in 2015–16. The sanctions on Nepal have been in the form of trade measures, with the exception of those in 2005, which related to arms and military. The objectives of the sanctioner have, ostensibly, been variously about democracy, human rights, and (foreign) policy change (Global Sanctions Data Base (GSDB-R4), LeBow College of Business, Drexel University, 2025). The 1989–1990 blockade lasted about 15 months and severely impacted Nepal's economy, as the country is landlocked and heavily dependent on India for trade routes; the blockade contributed to political unrest in Nepal and may ultimately have played a role in the restoration of democracy in 1990.

potentially large when we appreciate that trade and investment flows are (usually) intertwined.

Explanation #2

Definition:

The accounting framework discussed previously presents an opportunity for rationalising the yardstick of success. Though a diplomatic aim is discrete and unique, the *intermediate* goals are economic in nature, which are measurable as a continuum. Assessment of success can be a *granularised* metric in line with how sanctions erode the target's economic capability.

The measurement of success needs to be recast. Degrading an economy is a *process*, not an event. It is tenable that the sanctioner evaluates the success of the sanctions regime by an annual, dispassionate appraisal of the diminishment—in relation to a baseline—of the sanctioned country's economy (external viability, defence spending, GDP, credit outlook [commentary and rating], nutrition levels, health indicators, life expectancy, confidence surveys, etc.). Economic outcomes detrimental to the target can justify the policy of increasing sanctions and secondary sanctions, and not a reversal of policy by the sanctioner in short order, notwithstanding that the target has not *yet* been brought to heel.

Explanation #3

Despite ineffectiveness, the cost of exit from policy by sanctioners could be too costly (politically); or, the dual that little is gained by ending sanctions. In other words, once a sanctions regime comes into effect (and cost has been incurred by sanctioner for setting it up), the (marginal) cost sustained by the sanctioner, arguably, is small.

Voters in sanctioning countries are unaware of the economic cost (in domestic currency terms) to sanctioned and third countries. Neither sanctioning governments nor multilateral macro-financial institutions present and highlight relevant estimates, so voters in sanctioning countries apathetically support what their governments do. The blowback of sanctions on victims is invisible, unlike in physical wars. Without information on the economic outcomes of sanctions, voters, in effect, 'function in a void of indifference'.

Retain or shed a sanction?

A heuristic representation of the sanctioner's choice

Let V_t be the 'continuation value' to the sanctioner of a sanction on the target.

Consider the case where the sanctioner acts as if it were maximising in each period *t*, the expectation of the time-additive utility functional U_t below:

$$U_t = \sum_{i=0}^{\infty} \beta^i \, u(K_{t+i}), 0 < \beta < 1;\ u' > 0;\ u'' \leq 0;\ u'(0) = \infty \quad (2.1)$$

Where K_t are the sanctions on the target in period *t* and β is the discount factor.

We further use the following notation:

- F_t is the harm to the target if a sanction is retained

by the sanctioner. K_t and F_t are assumed to be linearly proportional to each other via the sanctions technology.

- G_t is the sanctioner's payoff for *shedding* a sanction. It comprises benefits from a reversal of countersanctions by the target on the sanctioner; plus elimination of self-harm; plus international goodwill; minus the loss of face.
- ρ_t is the return to the sanctioner of a sanction on the target.
- δ_t is the 'cost' to the sanctioner of leakage, expressed as per cent of harm to the target on account of the sanction (leakage undermines the value of a sanction to the sanctioner).
- $(\rho_t - \delta_t)\, F_t$ is the benefit to the sanctioner of retaining a sanction.

Rational intertemporal choice by the sanctioner means that the continuation value of a sanction retained by the sanctioner is constrained by the 'Euler equation' below, where E_t is the expectation operator conditional on information at time t.

$$\frac{V_t}{F_t} u'(k_t) = E_t \left\{ [F_t(\rho_t - \delta_t) + \max\{G_{t+1}, V_{t+1}\}] \frac{1}{F_{t+1}} \beta u'(k_{t+1}) \right\} \quad (2.2)$$

The equation brings out that the determination of the continuation value, to the sanctioner, of a sanction on the target requires the tool of option pricing.

Retaining a sanction on the target for the current period

means retaining the option of shedding it next period, should next period's payoff, G_{t+1}, exceed next period's continuation value.

Note that the 'strike price' that determines whether or not the option to shed is exercised next period, V_{t+1}, is itself uncertain at time t.

3

A STYLISED SYSTEMS APPROACH TO SANCTIONS, COUNTERMEASURES AND LEAKAGE

Do the restrictions, their relaxation and reimposition (gyrations or snap-backs) induce hysteresis (whiplash)?

ONE ASPECT THAT may benefit from an experimental conceptual depiction relates to: (i) the dynamics of the harm or cost to the sanctioned country ('deoxygenate'); (ii) the reaction of the sanctioned country to lessen the impact of sanctions; and (iii) important dimensions that lend themselves to be included in a formal model, viz., first, there is a delay between the time sanctions are imposed, with concomitant cost felt by the sanctioned country, and when mitigation measures become effective to reduce harm to the sanctioned country—conflated with the scope for leakage; secondly, the cost to the sanctioned country manifests differently when sanctions are removed or wound down ('reoxygenate') in comparison to when they are put in place—there is an element of *hysteresis*. This suggests that sanctions have enduring implications for the sanctioned country's welfare. Reversal does not make up for the loss of economic activity (or welfare).[1] It is striking that *The Research Handbook on Economic Sanctions*[2] does not have a single mention of hysteresis.

The model is in the form of a delay differential equation for the cost to the sanctioned country, and a functional relation for the hysteresis. Without sanctions a country is on a specific economic-financial profile. With a sanctions programme there is degradation of an economic or social activity of the sanctioned country, from some benchmark, measured by an economic variable, say, GDP, official foreign exchange reserves, the human and/or physical capital stock, etc. The sanctioned country is, inevitably, confronted with how much to reduce the impact.

When sanctions are activated from a 'cold start', they produce 'harm/cost/heat', g_y, measured by some economic variable, λ, for the sanctioned country. This

1 In a way, the harm to the sanctioned country is a mirror image of the payoff/benefit to the sanctioner—a 'positive' to its 'objective' function.

2 van Bergeijk, Peter A.G., ed., *The Research Handbook on Economic Sanctions*, Elgaronline, Northampton, MA, 2021.

depends on the quantum of decrease in the economic variable of interest. The sanctioned country, at some point, contingent on the extent of 'harm/cost/heat', implements (counter)measures for neutralising or circumventing sanctions. The extent of (counter)measures is captured/summarised/determined by a parameter $0 \leq \delta \leq 1$; counteracting sanctions is itself not costless for the sanctioner. The efficacy of the (counter)measures implemented by the sanctioned country to soften the 'heat/cost/harm' is denoted by g_c. See **Figure 3.1** for a diagrammatic depiction.

Figure 3.1 Schematic Setting of Sanctions, Countermeasures and Leakage

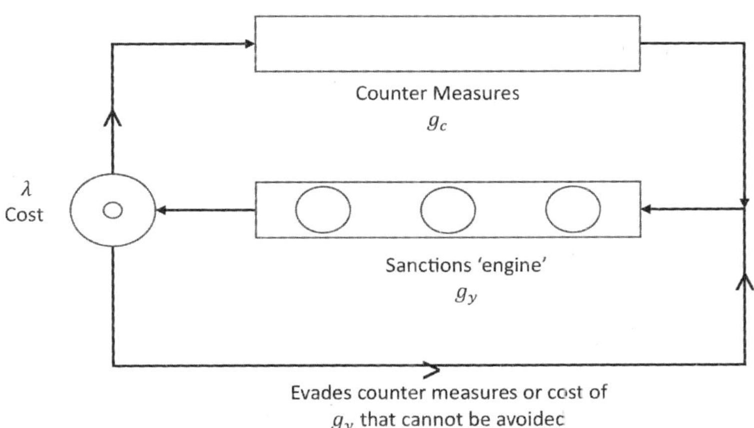

The asymmetry in the measure of decline in the economic variable that we are interested is that between reduction or mitigation of sanctions and their unabated continuation. This is the hysteresis behaviour, represented by hysteresis graph γ in **Figure 3.2**.

Figure 3.2: Hysteresis Curve of γ

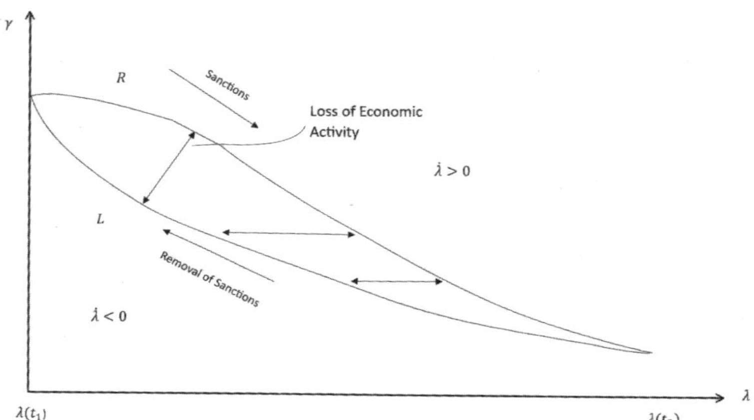

The function $\delta = \delta(t)$ is required to be a selection from the graph γ. In turn, γ depends on the economic variable measured of the harm or cost to the sanctioned country, γ, and on the rate of change $\dot{\lambda} = \lambda / dt$; that is:

$$\gamma = \gamma\ (\lambda,\ \dot{\lambda}) \tag{3.1}$$

In effect, γ depends only on the sign of $\dot{\lambda}$.

Hysteresis affects the dynamic behaviour as follows. When the initial state of the system $\{\lambda,\ \delta\}$ is on the curve R and the cost is rising, i.e., $\dot{\lambda} > 0$ (as sanctions intensity increases), the system will continue moving along the curve R. When the system is on curve L and the cost is decreasing with a reduction in sanctions intensity (or enhanced mitigation), i.e.,

$\dot{\lambda} < 0$, the system will continue moving along the curve L. When the cost rises with the system on R and then reverses, the system will move along the straight horizontal segment that connects curve R with curve L at constant δ. It will then continue moving up on L; an oscillatory pattern of sanctions imposition and relaxation is possible.

An obvious and systemic example of an economic variable that captures the hysteresis is what happens to the risk premium for investment in a country when sanctions are imposed and when they are lifted; it never quite goes back to the pre-sanctions level, at least over the period of interest.

The assumption that the motion is on horizontal segments represents the so-called 'generalised play' model.[3] Alternate choices of families of curves that fill the area between R and L, the hysteresis region, are possible. Based on the description above we denote by H_γ the 'generalised play hysteresis' operator so that, for a given (level of) economic variable of interest, the countermeasure is $\delta(t) = H_\gamma(\lambda(t))$.

We have to now address the issue of the delay that exists in the system. Let τ be the time it takes for the sanctioned country's countermeasures to kick off mitigation. The mitigating effect on the sanctioned country starts bearing fruit τ units of time later, which means that at time t the benefit of the countermeasures is from those in place at $t - \tau$.

The model consists of three elements: (a) the impact of sanctions equation; (b) the initial conditions; and (c) the

3 Visintin, A., 'Mathematical Models of Hysteresis', *Topics in Nonsmooth Mechanics,* J.J. Moreau, P.D. Panagiotopoulos, and G. Strang (eds.), Birkhäuser, 1988, pp. 295–323.

hysteresis domain and curves. (See Cahlon et al., 1997[4] and Zou et al., 1999[5] for proof and analogous details of the model below.)

g_y is the economic or social activity felt by the sanctioned country, as measured by λ.

g_c is the efficacy of the (counter) measures of the sanctioned country seeking to mitigate the sanctions.

Find a pair $\{\lambda, \delta\}$ such that:

$$\frac{d\lambda(t)}{dt} = g_y - g_c\delta(t - \tau);\ t \geq 0 \tag{3.2}$$

$$\delta(t) = H_\gamma\ (\lambda(t));\ -\tau \leq t \tag{3.3}$$

$$0 \leq \delta \leq 1$$

To complete the model, we have to impose the initial conditions:

$$\lambda(t) = \lambda_0(t) \text{ for } -\tau \leq t \leq 0 \tag{3.4}$$

$$\delta(-\tau) = \delta_0 \tag{3.5}$$

$g_c\delta(\mathrm{t} - \tau)$ is the extent of economic loss that is lessened by the sanctioned country's policies.

When $\delta = 1$, the sanctioned country attempts to considerably diminish the impact of the sanctions. When

---

4 Cahlon, B., D. Schmidt, M. Shillor, and X. Zou, 'Analysis of Thermostat Models', *European Journal of Applied Mathematics,* vol. 8, 1997, pp. 437–455.

5 Zou, X., J.A. Jordan, and M. Shillor, 'A Dynamic Model for a Thermostat', *Journal of Engineering Mathematics,* vol. 36, 1999, pp. 291–310.

$\delta = 0$, no (counter)measures are implemented and sanctions are highly effective.

It is reasonable to place an upper bound on δ, say, $\bar{\delta}$, such that $g_y \geq g_c\delta(t - \tau)$ for all $\delta < \bar{\delta}$ even as $g_y < g_c$.

Bells and Whistles

We can modify the model by introducing a distinct 'outside' leakage parameter, σ:

$$0 \leq \sigma \leq 1, \tag{3.6}$$

which enhances the sanctioned country's mitigation efforts, including help from a 'white knight' that aids to moderate the intensity of sanctions, or a sudden discrete change in the policy of the sanctioner. As shorthand, we can have a modified or an augmented δ:

$$\begin{aligned} &\delta^{aug} = \left(\sigma + \delta\left(t - \tau\right)\right) \\ &0 \leq \delta^{aug} \leq 1 \end{aligned} \tag{3.7}$$

To describe the conditions for oscillations, let $\tilde{\lambda}_L$ and $\tilde{\lambda}_R$ be the solutions of:

$$L(\tilde{\lambda}_L) = g_y/g_c;\ R(\tilde{\lambda}_R) = g_y/g_c, \tag{3.8}$$

respectively, and let ε be the minimum of the one-sided slopes of the hysteresis curves at these values, that is:

$$\varepsilon = min\{L'(\tilde{\lambda}_L - 0),\ L'(\tilde{\lambda}_L + 0),\ R'(\tilde{\lambda}_R - 0),\ R'(\tilde{\lambda}_R + 0)\},^6 \qquad (3.9)$$

where:

$$L' = \frac{dL}{d\lambda}; R' = \frac{dR}{d\lambda} \qquad (3.10)$$

If we assume $g_c \tau \varepsilon > 1/e$, then for every solution $\{\lambda, \delta\}$ to (3.2)–(3.5) such that λ is not eventually constant, λ oscillates about the interval $[\tilde{\lambda}_L, \tilde{\lambda}_R]$, and δ oscillates about $\delta^* = g_y/g_c$ (see corollary 3.3 in Cahlon et al., 1997).[7]

Some Applications of Oscillation Drivers

Iran

Iran lends itself to a useful application of the above framework, which brings together the dynamics and hysteresis inherent in the evolution ('flow and ebb') of sanctions on that country. The Iranian oil sector represents a critical case study in the impact of international sanctions on a resource-dependent economy. As one of the world's largest holders of proven oil

6 In Zou et al., 1999 the condition is simplified to:

$$\varepsilon = min\left\{\frac{dL}{d\lambda}(g_y / g_c), \frac{dR}{d\lambda}(g_y / g_c)\right\}.$$

(Zou, X., J.A. Jordan, and M. Shillor, 'A Dynamic Model for a Thermostat', *Journal of Engineering Mathematics*, vol. 36, 1999, pp. 291–310.)

7 Cahlon, B., D. Schmidt, M. Shillor, and X. Zou, 'Analysis of Thermostat Models', *European Journal of Applied Mathematics*, vol. 8, 1997, pp. 437–455.

and gas reserves, Iran's ability to attract and deploy capital in its energy sector fundamentally shapes its economic trajectory and geopolitical position.

While there are many 'individual' sets of sanctions on Iran since the first in 1979—52 in total, of which 5 apply to groups of countries,[8] we can discern the following summary description and timeline of sanctions imposition, higher intensity, relaxation and reapplication:

- **1996–2000: Initial US Sanctions**
  The Iran–Libya Sanctions Act of 1996 limited US companies from investing more than US$ 20 million in Iran's energy sector. The impact was moderate, as European and Asian firms continued investing, but at cautious levels.
- **2009: Escalation, but pre-comprehensive sanctions**
  The National Iranian Oil Company (NIOC) was pursuing several major development projects, including work on phases of the South Pars gas field. International sanctions were present but had not yet reached their most severe levels.
- **2010–2015: Comprehensive International Sanctions (12 sets of sanctions)**
  - UN and expanded US sanctions created a near-complete

8 Global Sanctions Data Base (GSDB-R4), LeBow College of Business, Drexel University, 2025.

investment blockade (*see* Laub, 2015[9] for a useful description).[10; 11]

- EU oil embargo and SWIFT banking restrictions in 2012.
- **Key impacts:**
    - Major international oil companies (IOCs) exited projects.
    - Critical technology imports became unavailable.
    - New development projects stalled indefinitely.

- **Sanctions Lifted 2015–2018: Joint Comprehensive Plan of Action (JCPOA) Period**
    - Iran nuclear deal framework agreed in April 2015.
    - Multiple agreements signed with Total, Shell, Eni and others.
    - Technology transfers resumed after years of isolation.
    - Investment rebounded to US$4–5 billion annually.
    - But even during the JCPOA period, investors structured deals with accelerated payback periods of 5–7 years

9 Laub, Zachary, 'International Sanctions on Iran', *Council on Foreign Relations,* Washington, D.C., 2015,

10 United Nations Security Council Resolution number 1929, passed in June 2010, formed the legal basis for a coordinated international sanctions campaign. This was quickly followed by additional measures from the US and the EU, including the Comprehensive Iran Sanctions, Accountability, and Divestment Act (CISADA, July 2010) in the US and a series of EU directives targeting Iran's energy and financial sectors.

11 The most effective sanctions have been those with multilateral support, particularly when they included European partners and targeted banking and insurance sectors. By contrast, unilateral US sanctions, while impactful, have proven more susceptible to leakage through third-country relationships.

versus industry norms of 10–15 years, effectively increasing the cost of capital for Iran's oil sector.

- SWIFT messaging access was restored in 2016 for qualifying Iranian banks. Some specific sanctions on Iranian financial institutions were removed, and certain prohibitions on transactions were eased.
- While the technical legal barriers to correspondent banking were partially reduced, the practical reality saw very limited restoration of these relationships. Major international banks were reluctant to resume correspondent banking with Iranian institutions due to the complexity of remaining sanctions, compliance costs and reputational risks.

- **2018–Present: Renewed Sanctions (22 sets of sanctions)[12] instigating a more far-reaching role of 'white knights'**
  - Iran has been forced to rely on domestic investment capacity and upgradation of alliances with the 'white knights' (2019–2021): Russian partnership expansion,[13] and formalising of Chinese long-term agreement[14] in March 2021.[15]

---

12 The list of 'designations and updates' related to secondary sanctions on the OFAC website has 922 entries on Iran as of July 2025.

13 See: Samaan, Jean-Loup, 'Could the Russia-Iran Comprehensive Partnership Treaty Challenge Gulf Security?', *Middle East Council on Global Affairs,* Doha, 2025.

14 Relations were enhanced from the comprehensive strategic partnership in 2016 to the 25-year strategic cooperation agreement in 2021 (Scita, Jacopo, 'The China-Iran Agreement: A Blessing in Disguise for the JCPOA?', *The Institute for Peace and Diplomacy,* Ottawa, 2021.).

15 The China–Russia–Iran troika has been dubbed the 'Great Eurasian

- There are also smaller-scale arrangements with Iraq, Oman and others for technology sharing and border field development.
- Iranian banks were disconnected from SWIFT again in 2018 following the US withdrawal from the nuclear deal.

The trend(s) in investment in **Table 3.1**[16] broadly represents the essence of the theoretical framework. Investment levels are influenced by the full gamut of the sanctions' cycles, including financial strictures, as well as help from allies.

Partnership', the 'Eurasian Axis', etc.

16 There is a caveat. It is almost impossible, based on publicly available information, to generate a consistent time series for oil sector investment data on Iran from just one source (sanctions also affect data quality). This is why, out of ample caution, more than one series is tabulated using web-based sources and tools (the data sources cited in **Appendix 4** reflects the aforementioned); it is to convey that the evolution across the variables of interest is broadly similar—hence one can draw some comfort about the trends.

Table 3.1: Iran: Harm, λ_{inv}, to investment in the oil sector since 2009[17]

Year	Investment US$ billion (international data sources) (1)	*Decline* from 2009 level (2)	Investment US$ billion (Iran data sources) (3)	*Decline* from 2009 level (4)	Investment/ GDP (per cent) (5)	*Decline* from 2009 level (6)
2009	15–18	–	20–22	–	3.98	–
2010	10–12	5	14–15	6.5	2.26	1.72
2011	6–8	9	10–12	10	1.11	2.87
2012	4–5	11.5	7–8	13.5	0.70	3.28
2013	3–4	12	5–6	15.5	0.70	3.28
2014	3–4	13	4–5	16.5	0.76	3.22

(Table contd. on next page)

17 With respect to foreign investment in the oil sector, the fluctuations are even sharper, but magnitudes are smaller, as one would expect. The most reliable estimates suggest:1996–2000: approximately US$1–2 billion annually in foreign investment; 2001–2005: increased to US$3–5 billion annually as oil prices rose; 2006–2009: peaked at roughly US$6–8 billion annually; 2010–2015: dropped to US$1–3 billion annually during sanctions; 2016–2017: brief recovery to US$4–5 billion after JCPOA; and 2018–2024: declined again to approximately US$1–3 billion under renewed sanctions.

Year	Investment US$ billion (international data sources) (1)	*Decline* from 2009 level (2)	Investment US$ billion (Iran data sources) (3)	*Decline* from 2009 level (4)	Invest-ment/ GDP (per cent) (5)	*Decline* from 2009 level (6)
2015	4–5	11.5	5–6	15.5	1.10	2.88
2016	6–7	9	8–9	12.5	1.42	2.56
2017	8–10	7	11–12	9.5	1.84	2.14
2018	5–6	10.5	7–8	13.5	1.38	2.60
2019	3–4	12.5	5–6	15.5	1.05	2.93
2020	2–3	13.5	3–4	17.5	0.95	3.03
2021	3–4	12.5	5–6	15.5	0.91	3.07
2022	4–5	11.5	6–7	14.5	1.14	2.84
2023	5–6	10.5	8–9	12.5	1.36	2.62
2024	6–7	10	10–12	10	1.57	2.41

Source: See **Appendix 4**.

Perhaps the most significant structural change has been the transformation in investment sources as secondary and financial sanctions tightened. Prior to comprehensive sanctions, IOCs provided approximately 60–70 per cent of capital investment in Iran's oil sector, with domestic sources accounting for the remainder. By 2014, this ratio had effectively inverted, with domestic sources providing an estimated 75–80 per cent of total investment.

During the JCPOA period (2015–2018), international participation briefly increased but never exceeded 40 per cent of total investment. Following the reimposition of sanctions in 2018, foreign participation again declined sharply, with only Chinese and Russian firms maintaining significant positions.[18]

A similar pattern to that of investment is found in annual oil production data, presented in **Table 3.2**.

18 From 2020 onwards, estimated investment by China and Russia has been rising.2020: US$600–800 million by China, US$500–700 million by Russia; 2024: US$2.5–3.5 billion by China, US$1–1.5 billion by Russia.

Table 3.2: Iran: Harm, λ_{prod}, to oil production since 2010

Year	Production in million barrels per day (bpd)	*Decline* from 2010 level
2010	4.3	–
2011	4.2	0.1
2012	3.7	0.6
2013	3.2	1.1
2014	3.1	1.2
2015	3.2	1.1
2016	3.7	0.6
2017	3.8	0.5
2018	3.6	0.7
2019	2.4	1.9
2020	2.0	2.3
2021	2.4	1.9
2022	2.5	1.8
2023	2.7	1.6
2024	3.0	1.3

Source: OPEC reports, IEA data, EIA statistics and other energy industry publications.

The data related to investment suggest that while sanctions successfully restricted access to international capital and technology, Iran has developed adaptive (workaround) band-aid strategies—represented by δ (equation 3.3) in the formal model—that have enabled partial recovery of investment flows in recent years, primarily through domestic financing mechanisms and distinct partnerships with non-Western powers (the 'Axis of Resistance'), denoted by parameter σ (equation 3.6).[19] These include:

(i) Barter and commodity-based financing whereby banks facilitate complex barter arrangements, by directly exchanging oil exports for equipment, technology or services needed for upstream development. This circumvents traditional payment systems and reduces reliance on US dollar-denominated transactions that could trigger secondary sanctions.
(ii) Multi-currency settlement systems have been exploited by Iranian banks using sophisticated currency swap mechanisms and bilateral payment arrangements with partner countries, allowing oil trade to occur in local currencies or through alternative settlement systems that bypass SWIFT and other Western financial infrastructure.[20]

The hysteresis effect, as illustrated by the dot plots (**Figures 3.3** and **3.4**, using **Figure 3.2** as template), is maintainable; the loss on account of the sanctions is not made up in full when sanctions relief comes to pass—for instance, the period

19 An unintended consequence of sanctions has been the development of domestic capabilities within Iran's oil industry. Faced with international isolation, Iran has invested significantly in domestic manufacturing of basic oil equipment; training of technical specialists within Iranian universities; and, creation of domestic service companies.

20 These mechanisms, while less efficient than standard international financing, have enabled Iran to maintain minimal investment levels even during periods of maximum sanctions pressure.

2015–2018 (the gap between the two curves is a measure of this). Adaptations come at significant cost to efficiency, growth potential and technical development—costs that may persist after sanctions are eventually lifted.

Figure 3.3: Iran, Investment in the Oil Sector (Harm; Column [2] in Table 3.1)

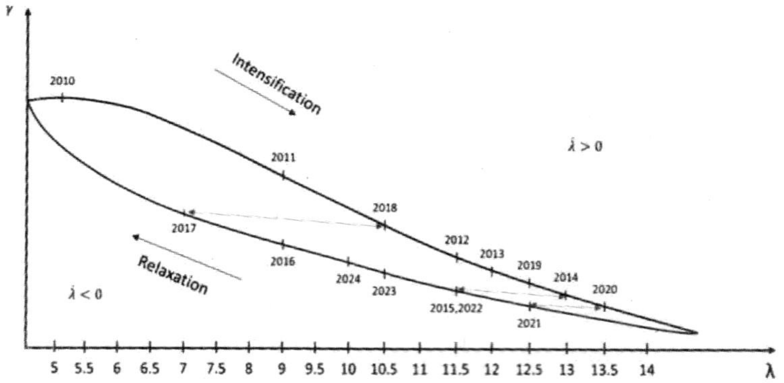

Figure 3.4: Iran, Oil Production (Harm)

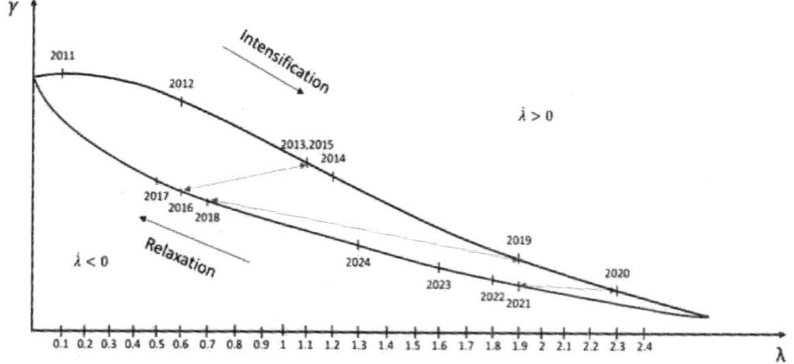

The contrast between the sanctions and non-sanctions periods has several dimensions:

1. **Enduring higher operational costs**:
   (i) *Country risk premium*: Investment analysts typically apply a 3–5 per cent additional risk premium specifically for Iran projects even during non-sanctioned periods
   (ii) *Insurance costs*: Marine and investment insurance for Iran projects commanded 30–40 per cent higher premiums even when sanctions were lifted, directly impacting project economics.
2. **Recovery speed**: When sanctions lift, investment responds within 6–12 months—but this does not mean that it reaches pre-sanctions level—as companies rush to secure position in Iran's resource-rich market.
3. **Investment magnitude**: Typically, 2–3 times higher investment during non-sanctioned periods.
4. **Project continuity**: Sanctions create a 'stop–start' dynamic that is particularly damaging for long-term projects that require consistent investment.
5. **Technological gap**: Each sanctions period widens the technological gap between Iran and global standards, requiring more investment when sanctions are (or, will be) lifted.

Belarus

Belarus has experienced cycles of international sanctions since 2005, reflecting broader patterns of authoritarian consolidation and geopolitical realignment. Initially imposed following the flawed 2004 referendum and subsequent electoral irregularities, Western sanctions primarily targeted individual officials through asset freezes and travel restrictions.

A notable period of relaxation occurred in 2015–2016 when the EU suspended most measures in response to political prisoner releases and Belarus's constructive role in Ukraine peace negotiations.

The sanctions regime intensified following the disputed 2020 presidential election and subsequent crackdown on opposition movements. The forced diversion of Ryanair flight 4978 in May 2021 catalysed unprecedented sectoral sanctions, particularly targeting Belarus's critical potash industry, which historically represented about 20 per cent of export revenues. Lithuania's decision to block Belarusian potash transit through Klaipėda port, which handled 95 per cent of exports, has been a logistical disruption that has forced Belarus towards alternative routes via Russian infrastructure, increasing transportation costs and market dependence on China and India. These measures effectively severed Belarus from Western markets, with potash exports declining from 6.3 million tonnes in 2019 to 1.6 million tonnes by 2023.[21]

---

21 Sanctions targeting Belarus's potash industry had the most dramatic quantifiable impact on the country's economy. Belarus transformed from a modest potash exporter in the early 2000s to one of the world's major suppliers by 2019, before sanctions severely constrained its export capabilities starting in 2021. Before sanctions Belarus was the world's third-largest potash producer, accounting for about 20 per cent of global supply. After the 2021 EU sectoral sanctions specifically targeting potash, the value of potash exports fell from approximately US$3 billion annually to under US$1 billion. While global potash prices initially rose due to supply constraints (benefiting Belarus somewhat), the country

Secondary sanctions pressure has led to a reduction in the willingness of Western banks to process Belarusian transactions. There is prohibition on EU and US financial institutions from providing services to designated Belarusian banks, and restrictions on correspondent banking relationships with Western financial institutions. While not completely excluded from SWIFT, unlike some Russian banks, several Belarusian banks face limited access to international payment systems.

Capital market curbs include an EU bar on providing investment services and activities to Belarusian entities. There are checks on trading in Belarusian government bonds and securities, and caveats on providing insurance and reinsurance services. Foreign exchange controls have entailed asset freezes targeting the National Bank of Belarus reserves held in Western jurisdictions, controls on foreign currency transactions for designated entities, and limitations on access to US dollar and Euro financing.[22]

The evolution of external reserves 'funnels' the impact of export-related and financial market sanctions—traversing intensity and relaxation (see **Appendix 5** for a description of the *granular* timeline of the gyrations in the sanctions regime since 2005). The impacts can be discerned by the import coverage ratio of Belarus' official foreign exchange reserves (**Table 3.3**).

---

was forced to sell at significant discounts (30–40 per cent below market rates) to alternative buyers like China and India.

22 Belarus has had to endure sustained economic pressure despite efforts to maintain macroeconomic stability through closer integration with Russian financial systems and trade networks.

Table 3.3: Belarus: Harm, λ_{forex}, to foreign exchange reserves import cover ratio since 2009

Year	Import cover ratio in months	*Decline* from 2009 level
2009	2.2	–
2010	1.6	0.6
2011	1.9	0.3
2012	1.9	0.3
2013	1.6	0.6
2014	1.3	0.9
2015	1.4	0.8
2016	1.8	0.4
2017	2.2	0.0
2018	1.9	0.3
2019	2.5	-0.3
2020	2.3	-0.1
2021	2.1	0.1
2022	2.0	0.2
2023	1.9	0.3
2024	2.0	0.2

Source: World Bank

Analogous to **Figures 3.3** and **3.4** for Iran, the dot plot for Belarus is presented in Figure **3.5** below:[23]

23 The data points for 2019 and 2020 are not plotted, as they are not consistent with the theoretical structure (admittedly a lacuna for this specific illustrative exercise of applying the model).

Figure 3.5: Belarus, Import Cover (Harm)

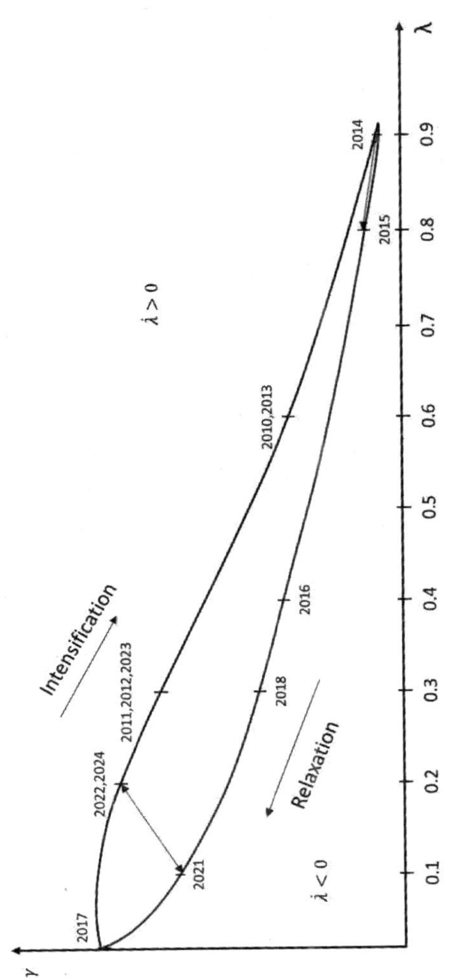

4

MORE SANCTIONS MAY NOT ALWAYS WORK: ROLE OF STRATEGIC IMPEDERS AND STRATEGIC REINFORCERS

ALTHOUGH OFFICIALS FROM sanctioning countries do not publicly admit, they acknowledge in private that they are not clear about the success (even directionally) of additional sanctions, i.e., the *marginal* effectiveness of further sanctions, due to the knock-on effects and reactions of stakeholders. The 'observed' tactical incoherence (a haphazard clutter) is not surprising given the multilayered characteristics of sanctions and secondary sanctions (like a 'drone swarm') in a complex environment;[1] there are information-sharing gaps, viz., even while agencies coordinate, they do not always have complete visibility into each other's ongoing sanctions designation processes, potentially leading to duplicative efforts or contradictory signals to the private sector.

1 The architecture of sanctions programmes, *prima facie*, points towards distinct regulatory philosophies and operational objectives, with each agency maintaining criteria for entity designation.

Consider the broad categories of sanctions by the US on China:[2;3;4]

- **Chinese Military-Industrial Complex Companies (CMIC)**: Around 60–80 plus companies designated for investment restrictions.
- **Entity List**: Several hundred Chinese entities (not all military-related).

---

2 Multiple agencies are responsible for sanctions. For instance, in the US: the Department of Treasury, the Department of Commerce and the Department of Defense. It does not take much for powerful agencies to work at cross purposes. The Entity List is maintained by the Department of Commerce's Bureau of Industry and Security, which focuses on export controls and technology transfer restrictions. The Special Designated Nationals and Blocked Persons List is administered by the Department of Treasury's OFAC, which handles comprehensive economic sanctions and asset freezing measures. The Department of Defence determines which technologies require export controls. The US Congress can impose sanctions through legislation, which requires passage by both chambers and either presidential signature or a veto override. Once enacted into law, these sanctions are binding. Examples include the Iran Sanctions Act, 1996 and various Russia-related sanctions laws.

3 The list of 'designations and updates' on the OFAC website has, as of July 2025, 284 entries related to China (see *Chapter 1* for discussion and more data on secondary sanctions). The most affected sectors are telecommunications (Huawei, ZTE, China Mobile), aerospace and defence contractors, surveillance technology companies, semiconductor and AI companies with military applications, and shipbuilding and maritime companies.

4 See Chorzempa et al., (2024) for a new data set on China. (Chorzempa, Martin, Mary E. Lovely, and Christine Wan, 'The Rise of US Economic Sanctions on China: Analysis of a New PIIE Dataset', *Policy Brief 24-14,* Peterson Institute for International Economics, 2024.)

- **OFAC Special Designated Nationals and Blocked Persons (SDN) List**: Dozens of Chinese individuals and entities.
- **Unverified List**: Additional Chinese companies with restricted access.

It is likely that several hundred Chinese entities face, directly or indirectly, some form of US secondary sanctions across all programmes, though the exact number fluctuates as companies are added or removed. Sanctions enforcement increasingly recognises the interconnected nature of global commercial networks, where entities from non-target countries may nonetheless warrant designation based on their functional role in undermining broader sanctions objectives, rather than their direct relationship with the primary country of concern.

Chinese entities frequently appear on the SDN List not primarily through China-focused sanctions programmes, but rather as collateral designations under sanctions regimes targeting third countries. This pattern emerges when Chinese entities assume what might be characterised as intermediary or facilitative roles—functioning as alternative channels or strategic enablers that potentially circumvent or dilute the intended impact of existing sanctions frameworks. Such entities may serve as conduits for sanctioned actors in other jurisdictions,[5] thereby weakening the structural integrity of established sanctions architectures.

5 The EU tends to coordinate with the US on some China sanctions but maintains its own legal framework and decision-making process, often resulting in fewer and less comprehensive China-specific sanctions compared to the US approach.

A corollary, from discussion and data in the first two chapters, is that things are not quite working up to the envisaged level of the stated and publicised goals of sanctioners.

The level of sanctions imposed by a country can change strategies elsewhere through reaction functions. The heterogeneous implications of the reactions, of sanctioners and targets/victims are multidimensional, as also across two 'geographies/theatres/markets', and, therefore, perhaps more subtle than *prima facie* is the case.

We set out to explore some of these 'interlinkages' in a heuristic, and stylised, formal simple example.[6] The attempt delves into the implications of measures like increasing the level of sanctions and imposing secondary sanctions, by transposing models of oligopolistic behaviour in product markets,[7] with suitable reinterpretations, into an illustrative sanctions context. It is found that the impact on (cross-variable) *marginal* (as opposed to actual) payoffs play an important role, specifically, whether sanctions and countersanctions/countermeasures ('drone wall') are, respectively, *strategic impeders* (inhibitors) or *strategic reinforcers* (stimulants). There is the prospect of additional or more intense sanctions leading to countermeasures that can (potentially) undermine payoff(s) of the sanctioner. Ambiguity is not rare. The question

6 The rigorous equilibrium derivations characteristic of game theory is eschewed in this illustrative exercise. Conditions required for Nash equilibrium are assumed. Liberty is taken and convenient assumptions are also imposed in the example for tractability.

7 Bulow, Jeremy, John Geanakoplos, and Paul Klemperer, 'Multimarket Oligopoly: Strategic Substitutes and Complements', *Journal of Political Economy*, vol. 93, 1985, pp. 488–511.

arises: are regular announcements of new sanctions an exercise in public relations ('we are on the job, doing something'), or made to create an atmosphere of fear through disorder?

The following notation is used:

U^S : payoff function of sanctioner/targeter.

U^T : payoff function of target.

Sanctioner chooses $\boldsymbol{x} = \{x_1^S, x_2^S\}$ for imposing cost on target and gain for itself. These can be thought of as the level or intensity of sanctions.

x_1^S : denotes the level of sanctions for maximising gain through engagement in the specific sector of the target (country 1). It impacts the payoff of both countries.[8]

x_2^S : level of sanctions by the sanctioner that affects only its geography (it is, in a manner of speaking, a 'monopolist' in country 2 in the sector of interest). We assume that in country 2, $x_2^S = k_2^S$.

x_1^T : denotes the level of countermeasures (or offsets) by the target (victim).

y : 'booster/kicker' (force multiplier) to the sanctioner's payoff from imposing, say, secondary sanctions on third country(ies)/collateral victims, to get them to support its primary sanctions (for example, intensification of (technological) export controls, curb input exports) on the target—instil fear in third countries to behave or threaten

8 As they interact by undercutting the 'competition', or by intensification of controls to undermine the target's capacity to engage or be viable in a specific sector.

them for violating sanctions on target. (Akin to a 'mafia' shakedown!)

B_1^S: is benefit to the sanctioner's objectives from applying pressure on target country, say, by way of degrading the target's influence in the sector of interest via engagement in the target country.

B_2^S: is value to the sanctioner, generated domestically, after imposing strictures on target.[9]

C^S: is composite cost, tangible and intangible, to the sanctioner of deploying x_1^S and x_2^S.

B_1^T: measures benefit to the target on account of implementing a level of countermeasures to mitigate impact of sanctioner's action(s), for example, trade deflection, finding ways of reducing trade costs in the sector with countries that are not sanctioned, that is, legal circumvention measures.[10] After all, necessity is the mother of invention.

C^T: is cost to the target of countermeasures.

The two payoff functions, in simple form, are the following:

$$U^S\left(x_1^S, x_2^S, x_1^T, y\right) = B_1^S\left(x_1^S, x_1^T\right) + B_2^S\left(x_2^S\right) - C^S\left(x_1^S, x_2^S\right) + yx_1^S \tag{4.1}$$

$$U^T\left(x_1^S, x_1^T\right) = B_1^T\left(x_1^S, x_1^T\right) - C^T\left(x_1^S, x_1^T\right) \tag{4.2}$$

9 Can be due to (coercive) diplomatic measures to enhance business for itself in the sector.

10 Yalcin, Erdal, Gabriel Felbermayr, Heider Kariem, Aleksandra Kirilakha, Ohyun Kwon, Constantinos Syropoulos, and Yoto V. Yotov, 'The Global Sanctions Data Base-Release 4: The Heterogeneous Effects of the Sanctions on Russia', *The World Economy*, 2025.

We assume that the functions are conventionally well behaved in terms of differentiable concave payoffs, convex costs etc. The sanctioner chooses a tuple $\{x_1^S, x_2^S\}$, that impinges on both countries. Simultaneously, the target chooses (defensive) countermeasures, x_1^T, for its economy/sector (that only helps it directly domestically). The following first-order conditions must be satisfied:

$$\frac{\partial U^S}{\partial x_1^S} = \frac{\partial B_1^S}{\partial x_1^S} - \frac{\partial C^S}{\partial x_1^S} + y = 0 \tag{4.3}$$

$$\frac{\partial U^S}{\partial x_2^S} = \frac{\partial B_2^S}{\partial x_2^S} - \frac{\partial C^S}{\partial x_2^S} = 0 \tag{4.4}$$

$$\frac{\partial U^T}{\partial x_1^T} = \frac{\partial B_1^T}{\partial x_1^T} - \frac{\partial C^T}{\partial x_1^T} = 0 \tag{4.5}$$

If we want to analyse the implication of an increase in y as a proxy for more strict (exogenous) secondary sanctions, we have to totally differentiate the first-order conditions:

$$\frac{\partial^2 U^S}{\partial x_1^S \partial x_1^S} dx_1^S + \frac{\partial^2 U^S}{\partial x_1^S \partial x_2^S} dx_2^S + \frac{\partial^2 U^S}{\partial x_1^S \partial x_1^T} dx_1^T + \frac{\partial^2 U^S}{\partial x_1^S \partial y} dy = 0 \tag{4.6}$$

$$\frac{\partial^2 U^S}{\partial x_2^S \partial x_1^S} dx_1^S + \frac{\partial^2 U^S}{\partial x_2^S \partial x_2^S} dx_2^S + \frac{\partial^2 U^S}{\partial x_2^S \partial x_1^T} dx_1^T + \frac{\partial^2 U^S}{\partial x_2^S \partial y} dy = 0 \tag{4.7}$$

$$\frac{\partial^2 U^T}{\partial x_1^T \partial x_1^S} dx_1^S + \frac{\partial^2 U^T}{\partial x_1^T \partial x_1^T} dx_1^T = 0 \tag{4.8}$$

The equations can be further simplified by noting that $\partial U^S / \partial y = x_1^S$. Therefore, $\partial^2 U^S / \partial x_1^S \partial y = 1$, and $\partial^2 U^S / \partial x_2^S \partial y = 0$ as the level of sanctions chosen are (at the margin, assumed to be) independent across the two 'geographies':[11]

$$\begin{bmatrix} \frac{\partial^2 U^S}{\partial x_1^S \partial x_1^S} & \frac{\partial^2 U^S}{\partial x_1^S \partial x_2^S} & \frac{\partial^2 U^S}{\partial x_1^S \partial x_1^T} \\ \frac{\partial^2 U^S}{\partial x_2^S \partial x_1^S} & \frac{\partial^2 U^S}{\partial x_2^S \partial x_2^S} & \frac{\partial^2 U^S}{\partial x_2^S \partial x_1^T} \\ \frac{\partial^2 U^T}{\partial x_1^T \partial x_1^S} & 0 & \frac{\partial^2 U^T}{\partial x_1^T \partial x_1^T} \end{bmatrix} \begin{bmatrix} dx_1^S \\ dx_2^S \\ dx_1^T \end{bmatrix} = \begin{bmatrix} -dy \\ 0 \\ 0 \end{bmatrix} \qquad (4.9)$$

We assume that the equilibrium is locally strictly stable, which implies that the determinant |U| of the matrix U is negative.

We also assume that the choice variable of the sanctioner (level of sanctions) and that of the target (level of countermeasures) have the plausible signs: $\partial U^S / \partial x_1^T < 0$ and $\partial U^T / \partial x_1^S < 0$ (sanctions and countermeasures are ['first-order'] impeders).

The following comparative statics can be extracted by solving for the three variables: dx_1^S / dy, dx_2^S / dy and dx_1^T / dy.

11 We can think of them, from the perspective of the sanctioner, as 'outward' facing and 'inward' facing, respectively. This 'sleight of hand' is not required to make the problem tractable with sequential decisions of sanctions where the sanctioner is able to, by definition, precommit to x_1^S.

a. $dx_1^S / dy > 0$.

b. sign (dx_2^S / dy) depends on a combination of whether x_1^S and x_2^S enjoy 'joint efficiencies' or 'joint inefficiencies', x_2^S and x_1^T are strategic reinforcers or strategic impeders, and x_1^T and x_1^S are strategic reinforcers or strategic impeders. The prefix 'strategic' is necessary as the reference is on the impact on the marginal payoff(s). There are eight possibilities for the sign of (dx_2^S / dy); see **Table 4.1**:

Table 4.1: Complexity

$(\partial^2 U^S / \partial x_2^S \partial x_1^S) > 0$	$(\partial^2 U^S / \partial x_2^S \partial x_1^T) < 0$	$(\partial^2 U^T / \partial x_1^T \partial x_1^S) < 0$	+ve
$(\partial^2 U^S / \partial x_2^S \partial x_1^S) > 0$	$(\partial^2 U^S / \partial x_2^S \partial x_1^T) > 0$	$(\partial^2 U^T / \partial x_1^T \partial x_1^S) < 0$	?
$(\partial^2 U^S / \partial x_2^S \partial x_1^S) > 0$	$(\partial^2 U^S / \partial x_2^S \partial x_1^T) < 0$	$(\partial^2 U^T / \partial x_1^T \partial x_1^S) > 0$	?
$(\partial^2 U^S / \partial x_2^S \partial x_1^S) > 0$	$(\partial^2 U^S / \partial x_2^S \partial x_1^T) > 0$	$(\partial^2 U^T / \partial x_1^T \partial x_1^S) > 0$	+ve
$(\partial^2 U^S / \partial x_2^S \partial x_1^S) < 0$	$(\partial^2 U^S / \partial x_2^S \partial x_1^T) < 0$	$(\partial^2 U^T / \partial x_1^T \partial x_1^S) < 0$	?
$(\partial^2 U^S / \partial x_2^S \partial x_1^S) < 0$	$(\partial^2 U^S / \partial x_2^S \partial x_1^T) > 0$	$(\partial^2 U^T / \partial x_1^T \partial x_1^S) < 0$	-ve
$(\partial^2 U^S / \partial x_2^S \partial x_1^S) < 0$	$(\partial^2 U^S / \partial x_2^S \partial x_1^T) < 0$	$(\partial^2 U^T / \partial x_1^T \partial x_1^S) > 0$	-ve
$(\partial^2 U^S / \partial x_2^S \partial x_1^S) < 0$	$(\partial^2 U^S / \partial x_2^S \partial x_1^T) > 0$	$(\partial^2 U^T / \partial x_1^T \partial x_1^S) > 0$	?

c. *sign* $(dx_1^T / dy,)$ depends on *sign* $(\partial^2 U^T / \partial x_1^T \partial x_1^S)$, that is whether x_1^T and x_1^S are strategic reinforcers (sign is positive) or strategic impeders (sign is negative).

Given the heterogeneous possibilities derived above, it should not be a surprise that there is the prospect of a decrease in payoff of the sanctioner as it ratchets up the level of sanctions on the target. The total effect of an additional secondary sanction, Δy, on the sanctioner's payoff is:

$$(\Delta y)\frac{dU^S}{dy} = (\Delta y)\left(\frac{\partial U^S}{\partial x_1^S}\frac{dx_1^S}{dy} + \frac{\partial U^S}{\partial x_2^S}\frac{dx_2^S}{dy} + \frac{\partial U^S}{\partial x_1^T}\frac{dx_1^T}{dy} + \frac{\partial U^S}{\partial y}\right) \quad (4.10)$$

The first-order conditions imply that the first two expressions in brackets on the right-hand side equal zero. If the strategic effect, (dx_1^T / dy), is positive (that is, x_1^T and x_1^S are strategic reinforcers) assuming reasonably that $(\partial U^S / \partial x_1^T)$ is negative, then dU^S / dy can be negative (it depends on the size of the last term in the equation above; that is if $\partial U^S / \partial y$ (> 0) is 'sufficiently small'). If the strategic effect, (dx_1^T / dy), is negative (that is, x_1^T and x_1^S are strategic impeders), again assuming reasonably that $(\partial U^S / \partial x_1^T)$ is negative, then dU^S / dy will be positive (as the last term in the equation above is also positive).

Let us analyse the sequential case—possibly a more realistic description of the real world—where the sanctioner can pre-commit to the level of sanctions in the target country. The modification is that instead of the first equilibrium condition being $\partial U^S / \partial x_1^S = 0$, it instead becomes $dU^S / dx_1^S = 0$. The implications of having sequential decisions can be seen from examining the first-order condition:

$$\frac{dU^S}{dx_1^S} = \frac{\partial U^S}{\partial x_1^S} + \frac{\partial U^S}{\partial x_2^S}\frac{dx_2^S}{dx_1^S} + \frac{\partial U^S}{\partial x_1^T}\frac{dx_1^T}{dx_1^S} + \frac{\partial U^S}{\partial y}\frac{dy}{dx_1^S} = 0 \qquad (4.11)$$

We know from the second first-order condition (equation 4.4) that $\partial U^S / \partial x_2^S = 0$. Also, $dy / dx_1^S = 0$, so the total effect on sanctioner's payoff of an increase in x_1^S is $\partial U^S / \partial x_1^S$ plus a strategic term. The value of the strategic term $(\partial U^S / \partial x_1^T)(dx_1^T / dx_1^S)$ can be found by differentiating and solving the first-order equations (4.7) and (4.8) simultaneously, as before, with appropriate rearranging.[12] [13]

$$\begin{pmatrix} \frac{\partial^2 U^S}{\partial x_2^S \partial x_2^S} & \frac{\partial^2 U^S}{\partial x_2^S \partial x_1^T} \\ 0 & \frac{\partial^2 U^T}{\partial x_1^T \partial x_1^T} \end{pmatrix} \begin{pmatrix} dx_2^S \\ dx_1^T \end{pmatrix} = \begin{pmatrix} -\frac{\partial^2 U^S}{\partial x_2^S \partial x_1^S} dx_1^S \\ -\frac{\partial^2 U^T}{\partial x_1^T \partial x_1^S} dx_1^S \end{pmatrix} \qquad (4.12)$$

$\partial U^S / \partial x_1^T$ is negative provided that countermeasures reduce the sanctioner's payoff, which is the whole point. Turning to the second component of the strategic term, using equation 4.12:

$$sign\frac{dx_1^T}{dx_1^S} = sign\left[\frac{\partial^2 U^T}{\partial x_1^T \partial x_1^S}\right] \qquad (4.13)$$

---

12 Determinant is assumed to be non-zero to apply Cramer's method.

13 Note that since x_1^S is precommitted because of the sequential rollout, $(\partial^2 U^S / \partial x_2^S \partial y) = 0$.

If x_1^S and x_1^T are strategic impeders, $(\partial^2 U^T / \partial x_1^T x_1^S) < 0$, then $\partial U^S / \partial x_1^S < 0$ (in equation 4.11), so the sanctioner will choose x_1^S at a higher level than the point where the marginal benefit equals the marginal cost of increasing x_1^S. If x_1^S and x_1^T are strategic reinforcers, $(\partial^2 U^S / \partial x_1^T x_1^S) > 0$, then $\partial U^S / \partial x_1^S > 0$, hence the sanctioner will choose x_1^S at a lower level than the point where the marginal benefit equals the marginal cost of increasing x_1^S.

Let us describe some of the tensions, if not inconsistencies, that come about with multiple sanctions and secondary sanctions regimes, which is the theme of this chapter:

1. US on China

- **Market Competition Contradictions and Consolidation Effects:** Sanctions aimed at protecting US technological advantages for military applications sometimes push Chinese companies to develop—government sponsored—indigenous alternatives more quickly. Secondary sanctions that limit Chinese access to global supply chains can accelerate China's drive for technological self-sufficiency, potentially making it a stronger long-term competitor.
- **Financial System Access vs. Monitoring Capabilities:** Secondary sanctions that cut Chinese banks off from the Western financial system reduce US ability to monitor and track suspicious transactions. When Chinese financial institutions operate outside SWIFT and the US dollar systems, it becomes harder for authorities to detect sanctions evasion or illicit financial flows.

- **Technology Transfer vs. Economic Decoupling:** The US has imposed sanctions on Chinese tech companies like Huawei and Semiconductor Manufacturing International Corporation (SMIC) to prevent technology transfer, while simultaneously maintaining secondary sanctions that can push these companies towards closer relationships with other sanctioned countries; this can accelerate the formation of alternative technology *ecosystems* that exclude US influence entirely.[14]
- **Alliance Coordination Challenges:** US secondary sanctions on Chinese entities sometimes conflict with ally relationships. For example, threatening sanctions on European or Asian companies that do business with sanctioned Chinese firms can strain alliances that are crucial for broader China policy coordination.
- **Third-Country Leverage:** Secondary sanctions can push China to deepen relationships with other sanctioned countries (Russia, Iran, North Korea), creating a coalition of sanctioned states (Axis of Resistance) that may be more difficult to influence than addressing each country individually.
- **Overall Strategic Implications:** These dynamics suggest

14 'Nvidia says it is concerned that any advantage gained by Huawei in China could eventually spread into other markets, helping Huawei build a stronger foundation from which to compete around the world. […] Washington's efforts gave Chinese companies "the spirit, the energy and the government support to accelerate their development," said Huang, who attended a tech conference in Taipei last week. "All in all, the export control was a failure."' ('Nvidia's Chief Says U.S. Chip Controls on China Have Backfired', *The Seattle Times,* 26 May 2025, https://tinyurl.com/42za3vte. Accessed on 10 September 2025.).

that secondary sanctions, while creating short-term pressure, may be undermining long-term US leverage over China by reducing Chinese dependence on US-controlled systems and simultaneously incentivising and encouraging China's technological self-sufficiency, creating novel digital-economic networks that exclude US influence.

The cross-purposes highlight the complexity that when sanctions are combined with multiple secondary sanctions for immediate tactical gains, they can sometimes undermine broader strategic objectives.

There is another recently baked layer that makes the subject even murkier. As a sidebar, the current trade wars, trans-Pacific and trans-Atlantic, have had the inadvertent upshot that segments of sanctions policy—export controls on microchips, specifically—have become part of mainstream trade bargaining between the two 'elephants': 'For more than 40 years, China has sought to make US national security export controls a negotiable and transactional part of the trade relationship. They have finally succeeded. US allies will wonder why they should go along with tougher restrictions on their exports of high-tech goods to China (like semiconductor manufacturing equipment) when the US is prepared to trade them away. What export control concessions will China demand as part of any deal to be negotiated before the trade war ceasefire expires on August 11, or as part of a trip to China by President Trump later this year?'[15]

15 Padilla, Christopher, LinkedIn post, 2025, https://tinyurl.com/3uksfep2. Accessed on 10 September 2025.

2. US and the EU on Russia

- **Nord Stream 2 Pipeline**: The US imposed secondary sanctions on European companies involved in Nord Stream 2 construction, while the EU initially resisted these measures as extraterritorial overreach. This created tensions between allies and delayed coordinated action. The US sanctions actually pushed some European energy companies to *accelerate* completion before sanctions fully took effect.
- **Financial System Fragmentation:**
  - **SWIFT vs. Alternative Systems**: While both the US and the EU excluded Russian banks from SWIFT, secondary sanctions pressure accelerated development of alternative payment systems, viz., the Cross-border Interbank Payment System (China) and System for Transfer of Financial Messages (Russia) that other countries now use to (partially) avoid US dollar-based transactions entirely—undermining long-term Western financial leverage.
  - **Cryptocurrency Adaptation**: Strict sanctions pushed Russia towards cryptocurrency and digital payment alternatives, which then became harder to monitor and control, reducing overall sanctions effectiveness.
- **Third-Country Relationships:**
  - **Turkey and India**: Secondary sanctions threats against countries buying Russian energy kicked up diplomatic tensions with key partners. Turkey's continued Russian gas purchases and India's oil imports induced policy dilemmas where enforcing secondary sanctions would

damage relationships with strategically important non-aligned countries.

- ○ **China Banking**: US secondary sanctions on Chinese banks dealing with Russia have been applied selectively to avoid broader economic disruption, creating *inconsistent* enforcement (leakage) that reduces the deterrent effect.

3. US and the EU on Iran

- **INSTEX vs. US Financial Pressure:** The EU created the Instrument in Support of Trade Exchanges (INSTEX) in 2019 to facilitate humanitarian trade with Iran while avoiding US sanctions. However, US secondary sanctions made banks and companies reluctant to use the mechanism, effectively neutering the EU's policy tool and forcing European policy into alignment with US preferences rather than EU strategic objectives.
- **China–Russia–Iran Axis:** Secondary sanctions that isolated Iran from Western financial systems accelerated its integration with Chinese and Russian economic networks. This contributed to a sanctions-resistant bloc that became harder to influence and potentially more threatening to Western interests than Iran operating alone.
- **Nuclear Programme Acceleration:** Sanctions aimed at constraining Iran's nuclear programme sometimes incentivised the opposite behaviour. When economic pressure became severe enough, Iran began exceeding uranium enrichment limits and reducing International Atomic Energy Agency (IAEA) cooperation, using nuclear

escalation as leverage against sanctions—essentially making the nuclear problem worse in the short term.

- **JCPOA Implementation Period (2015–2018):** The most significant example occurred during the Iran nuclear deal implementation. The EU maintained that the JCPOA was working and wanted to preserve economic engagement with Iran, while the US reimposed comprehensive sanctions in 2018. US secondary sanctions threatened European companies doing legitimate business with Iran under the JCPOA framework, undermining EU policy objectives and creating transatlantic tensions.
- **Regional Proxy Strategy:** Economic sanctions pushed Iran towards asymmetric responses through regional proxies (Houthis, Hezbollah and Iraqi militias). This created security challenges that sometimes conflicted with other US and EU regional objectives, such as stability in Iraq, Yemen and Lebanon.

The conclusion is inescapable: is it even possible for sanctioners to be consistent with so many sanctions and secondary sanctions? Highly unlikely.

5

TIME TO DISENTANGLE (SMOG #2)

Beyond Performative Posturing by Multilateral 'Guardians'

INTERNATIONAL ORGANISATIONS LIKE the IMF, whose bailiwick includes spillovers and externalities as part of the surveillance function, provide scant informative estimates on sanctions, secondary sanctions, and countersanctions; a look at G20 communiqués of the last two years underscores the paucity of desire for transparency, no doubt settled by rarefied political arrangements at the global high table.[1] The G20 is almost

1 Work of technocratic multilateral organisations is supposed to inform the dialogue at the G20, but there does not seem to be a prominent workstream on sanctions—or, it is well hidden—while there are numerous ideating (drafting) groups on subjects of relatively peripheral worth.

apologetic on the topic of sanctions and its reverberations. **Table 5.1** below captures the global body's reticence:

Table 5.1: G20 Communiqués and Sanctions

Date	G20 presidency	Mention of sanctions	Length of statement/ communiqué (pages)
4th FMCBG Chair's Statement, October 2024	Brazil	0	1
3rd FMCBG Communiqué, July 2024	Brazil	0	12
Chair's Summary 1st FMCBG, February 2024	Brazil	0	4
Final FMCBG, October 2023 (Marrakesh)	India	0	7
Leaders' Declaration, September 2023	India	0	37
FMCBG Outcome Document and Chair's Summary, July 2023	India	1*	18
Leaders' Declaration, November 2022	Indonesia	2**	19
4th FMCBG, October 2022	Indonesia	3***	7
3rd FMCBG Chair's Summary, July 2022	Indonesia	1****	4

Extracts where sanctions are mentioned:

*Most members strongly condemned the war in Ukraine and stressed

that it is causing immense human suffering and exacerbating existing fragilities in the global economy constraining growth, increasing inflation, disrupting supply chains, heightening energy and food insecurity, and elevating financial stability risks. There were other views and different assessments of the situation and sanctions.
**Most members strongly condemned the war in Ukraine and stressed it is causing immense human suffering and exacerbating existing fragilities in the global economy—constraining growth, increasing inflation, disrupting supply chains, heightening energy and food insecurity, and elevating financial stability risks. There were other views and different assessments of the situation and sanctions.
We continue to support the carve out of humanitarian activities from sanctions and call on all nations to support this aim, including through current efforts at the UN.
***A few of these members noted that the sanctions against Russia do not target food. One G20 member expressed the view that the war in Ukraine and sanctions have impacted the global economy. One G20 member expressed the view that the sanctions are the main cause of the negative impacts on the global economy.
****One member expressed the view that the sanctions are adding to existing challenges.

Source: G20 (2022a,[2] 2022b,[3] 2023a,[4] 2023b,[5] 2024[6]).

Although tomes are written on policy spillovers and spillbacks by international macro-financial institutions,

2 G20, *Communiqué/Chair's Summary, Finance Ministers and Central Bank Governors,* Indonesia, July and October 2022a.

3 G20, *Leaders' Declaration,* Indonesia, November 2022b.

4 G20, *Communiqué/Chair's Summary, Finance Ministers and Central Bank Governors,* India, July and October 2023a.

5 G20, *Leaders' Declaration,* India, September 2023b.

6 G20, *Communiqué/Chair's Statement/Summary, Finance Ministers and Central Bank Governors,* Brazil, February, July and October 2024.

their explicit and dedicated research output on the *distinct* implications of sanctions, countersanctions, and the widespread fallout from secondary sanctions are, without exaggeration, missing in action.

It is noteworthy that on international splintering—a fashionable navel-gazing indulgence of the intelligentsia—the IMF's management in its remarks in June 2024 on *Navigating Fragmentation, Conflict, and Large Shocks,* does not feel the necessity of deploying any of the following terminology: sanctions, countersanctions, secondary sanctions, extraterritorial restrictions, spillovers, externalities. Remarkable omissions considering the title and the timing of the talk. By comparison, 'war' appears about two dozen times in the 15-page speech.[7]

While accepting that economic sanctions' effects are macroeconomic in nature, directly for target, and directly and indirectly for third parties, there is a dearth of *separate* analysis and credible estimates of economic losses for the sanctioned, adverse commercial and economic implications for the secondary-sanctioned, and third-party victims (see **Table 5.2**).

7 Gopinath, Gita, 'Navigating Fragmentation, Conflict, and Large Shocks', *NBU–NBP Annual Research Conference,* International Monetary Fund, Washington, D.C., 2024.

Table 5.2: Relevant 'Mentions' in IMF's World Economic Outlook (WEO)

Date	Sanctions	Counter-sanctions	Secondary sanctions	Spillover(s) (endured by bystanders/ third parties in the context of sanctions and secondary sanctions)	Spillover effect(s) (endured by bystanders/ third parties in the context of sanctions and secondary sanctions)	Externality(ies) (endured by bystanders/ third parties in the context of sanctions and secondary sanctions)
October 2024	1	0	0	28(0)	0	1(0)
July 2024	0	0	0	3(0)	0	0
April 2024	1	0	0	179(0)*	1(0)	2(0)
October 2023	5	1	0	33(0)	1(0)	1(0)
July 2023	0	0	0	4(0)	0	0
April 2023	6	0	0	73(0)**	4(0)	0
October 2022	8	0	0	24(0)	4(0)	0

(Table contd. on next page)

Date	Sanctions	Counter-sanctions	Secondary sanctions	Spillover(s)	Spillover effect(s)	Externality(ies)
July 2022	4	0	0	9(0)	0	0
April 2022	35	0	0	68(0)#	11(0)	2(0)

*An entire chapter on spillovers, but not in the context of sanctions.

**Two chapters with sections on spillovers, but not in the context of sanctions.

#Alludes to weaker demand in Asia from the Euro area because of the Ukraine and Russia war. Further, due to higher oil prices, domestic demand is also weak in Asia (e.g., Japan, India) (page 5). Otherwise, discussion is related to the COVID-19 lockdowns.

Source: International Monetary Fund (2022a,[8] 2022b,[9] 2022c,[10] 2023a,[11] 2023b,[12] 2023c,[13] 2024a,[14] 2024b,[15] 2024c[16]).

8 International Monetary Fund, *World Economic Outlook*, Washington, D.C., April 2022a.

9 International Monetary Fund, *World Economic Outlook*, Washington, D.C., July 2022b.

10 International Monetary Fund, *World Economic Outlook*, Washington, D.C., October 2022c.

11 International Monetary Fund, *World Economic Outlook*, Washington, D.C., April 2023a.

12 International Monetary Fund, *World Economic Outlook*, Washington, D.C., July 2023b.

13 International Monetary Fund, *World Economic Outlook*, Washington, D.C., October 2023c.

14 International Monetary Fund, *World Economic Outlook*, Washington, D.C., April 2024a.

15 International Monetary Fund, *World Economic Outlook*, Washington, D.C., July 2024b.

16 International Monetary Fund, *World Economic Outlook*, Washington, D.C., October 2024c.

By melding war with 'associated' sanctions (phrase used in the documents) the Fund's sleight of hand in its estimates of growth and trade implies that the war *and all* the sanctions are *one* source of shock and the ensuant diminution of welfare; fact is that they are not—sanctions and secondary sanctions are two classifiable policy choices by sanctioners, as is, to be fair, choice of war and countersanctions by the target.

Comprehensive and unbiased research on the ramifications of economic sanctions, primary and secondary, is necessary to create technocratic space for review and evaluation. The IMF's failure to illuminate is either conscious obfuscation or unconscious oversight (deeply unsettling either way); the deficient work in this area means the precise *incidence* of the economic consequences of the sanctions framework is overlooked.[17;18] It is a plausible suspicion that it would be disagreeable for sanctioners to pinpoint this as it pertains to *distribution* of the welfare loss attributable to their policies.[19] Both wars and sanctions are a 'tax', but who bears how much of the burden of the latter is deemed unimportant, thus overlooked; the Fund sidesteps and bypasses obvious dimensions of sanctions in its research work.

---

17 Conceptually the decomposition is straightforward. Use can be made of the following notation: the war/event/catalyst is x, a primary economic sanction on the target is y, and a secondary sanction on third parties is z (with modification y and z can be formulated as vectors, and a time dimension can be incorporated).

Say, W^T is a measure of the impact on the target, T (the sanctioned country):

$W^T = f(x, y, z)$

Total differentiation:

$dW^T = W^T_x(x, y, z).dx + W^T_y(x, y, z).dy + W^T_z(x, y, z).dz;$

(where the subscript denotes partial derivative with respect to the specific variable.)

Let W^{Row} denote a (consolidated) measure of the impact on all other economies because of economic and financial interlinkages with the target and execution of secondary sanctions:

$W^{Row} = f(y, z)$

Total differentiation:

$dW^{Row} = W^{Row}_y(y,z).dy + W^{Row}_z(y, z).dz$

Row can be trifurcated into sanctioner, developed countries and emerging economies to delineate incidence.

18 The IMF has suggested that sanctions-related financial fragmentation could reduce global GDP by 0.2–1.4 per cent in extreme scenarios, which would translate to hundreds of billions in annual costs.

19 There is a long history of Compensating Variation and Equivalent Variation concepts applied to a variety of policy comparisons.

The embarrassing possibility of sanctions *enhancing* economic welfare of sanctioners may not be purely conjectural. While the task may not be easy, given how Integrated Assessment Models (IAMs) for implications of climate change (an undertaking more complex than channels related to economic sanctions) are constructed, estimating the effects of (ever increasing) sanctions is eminently doable.

It is interesting that towards the bottom of page 5 in the April 2022 WEO the authors write: 'The fluid international situation means that quantitative forecasts are even more uncertain than usual. Yet some conduits through which the war and associated sanctions will affect the global economy seem relatively clear, even if their magnitudes are difficult to assess.'[20]

Nonetheless, in the scenario box on page 25, the 'delta or partial derivative' of a further *change* in sanctions is estimated:[21]

> The IMF's G20 model is used to explore the global macroeconomic implications of a scenario in which the sanctions on Russia arising from the war in Ukraine *escalate further* [my emphasis]. In the scenario sanctions are broadened mid-2022 to include additional embargoes on oil and gas and the disconnection of Russia from much of the global financial and trade system.

One can reasonably surmise that it is possible to calculate *exclusive* estimates of the effects of sanctions, countersanctions, and secondary sanctions, rather than conflate *all* the effects of the 'war *and* [my emphasis] associated sanctions'. The IMF

20 International Monetary Fund, *World Economic Outlook*, Washington, D.C., April 2022a, p. 5.

21 Ibid. p. 25.

has the wherewithal to do this work. The objectivity that it is supposed to bring to issues of externalities/spillovers behoves it to move ahead of functional pretension.

The World Bank's annual flagship World Development Report (WDR) ignores the subject *in toto* (World Bank, 2021,[22] 2022,[23] 2023,[24] 2024[25]). Across the last four editions, a word check reveals that 'sanctions' appear, in aggregate, eight times in reports that run into hundreds of pages, even as dozens of developing economies endure (collateral) consequences of sanctions. Only in one out of these eight instances, and that too in a footnote, is 'sanctions' contextualised with 'economic sanctions' as understood in this book.[26]

---

22 World Bank, *World Development Report: Data for Better Lives,* Washington, D.C., 2021.

23 World Bank, *World Development Report: Finance for an Equitable Recovery,* Washington, D.C., 2022.

24 World Bank, *World Development Report: Migrants, Refugees, and Societies,* Washington, D.C., 2023.

25 World Bank, *World Development Report: The Middle-Income Trap,* Washington, D.C., 2024.

26 'Sending remittances may also be complicated by sanctions and the impact of conflict on the origin country's financial system' (World Bank, *World Development Report: Migrants, Refugees, and Societies,* Washington, D.C., 2023.).

6

WHITHER RENMINBI INTERNATIONALISATION?

Not recognising and confronting softer issues makes it hard, but not impossible, to meaningfully advance the cause.

THE WEAPONISATION OF the US dollar—essentially censoring transactions for non-economic goals—has been the force multiplier of the West-sponsored sanctions and secondary sanctions regime (**Figure 1.1** in *Chapter 1* and **Table 2.3** in *Chapter 2*). Most financial sanctions are implemented by nations in North America and Europe, with these measures primarily directed at countries in Asia and Africa.[1]

Concomitantly, the expansion of Chinese geopolitical influence, leveraging its continental positioning across Asia and the strategic partnership with Russia to extend reach into European spheres, constitutes a significant multidimensional variable in contemporary international economic relations. The terrestrial infrastructure network sponsored by the Belt and Road Initiative (BRI) encompasses transcontinental connectivity extending through Africa via the Suez–Sinai corridor, fashioning integrated logistical pathways. The facilitation of financial and material assistance to multiple regional actors establishes a framework of spatially contiguous dependencies; this 'network' functions, depending on subjective, even prejudiced, viewpoints, as either a stabilising economic lifeline or a mechanism of graduated hegemonic control—either way, unprecedented *sui generis* adjunct structures.

As a corollary, with each report over the last decade or so of how third countries are affected by secondary sanctions, the Renminbi (RMB) as an alternative to the US dollar is 'talked up'. Here is a broad timeline:

2022–Present (Geopolitical Tensions and Reignition of the Trade War): Recent geopolitical developments and sanctions concerns have led to fresh discussions about RMB

---

1 Cipriani, Marco, Linda S. Goldberg, and Gabriele La Spada, 'Financial Sanctions, SWIFT, and the Architecture of the International Payments System', *Staff Reports,* no. 1047, Federal Reserve Bank of New York, 2023.

internationalisation, with China using the BRI to promote RMB usage and seizing on global trade disruptions to push its greater adoption.[2]

2018–2020 (Trade War Period): Renewed discussions emerged during US–China trade tensions, with some analysts suggesting that the RMB could challenge US dollar dominance.

2013–2016 (IMF SDR Inclusion Campaign): The most intensive period of reserve currency promotion came in the lead-up to the IMF decision in October 2016 to add the RMB to its Special Drawing Rights (SDR) basket.[3]

2009–2013 (Early Internationalisation Push): China launched its formal RMB internationalisation strategy around 2009, establishing currency swap agreements with multiple countries and allowing cross-border trade settlement in the currency.

2008–2009 (Global Financial Crisis): This was the first major period when the RMB gained serious attention as a potential

---

2 See: 'China Ramps Up Global Yuan Push, Seizing on Retreating Dollar', *Reuters*, 30 April 2025; and 'China Ramps Up Yuan Internationalisation under Belt and Road Initiative: During the Belt and Road Forum in Beijing That Ended on Wednesday, China's Policy Banks Signed a Series of Yuan-Denominated Loan Contracts with Foreign Lenders', *Reuters*, 19 October 2023.

3 There was debate around that time whether RMB met the criteria for inclusion in the SDR basket. It is because of its export performance rather than its role (source and destination) in global capital flows that this seems to have been justified; there are several emerging economies with a far more liberal and open capital account than China.

alternative reserve currency. The crisis exposed vulnerabilities in the US dollar-dominated system, and Chinese officials began discussing the need for a more diversified international monetary system.

Presently, the RMB has a modest role as an international currency. It would seem that the imprimatur of inclusion in the SDR basket has hardly mattered in macro-financial terms. By the gold-standard metric of its stake in official foreign exchange reserves, the share has not budged since 2020—2 per cent then, 2.1 per cent now—when some predicted that it would rise to 10 per cent by 2030.[4] Central banks during the extant uncertain times have pivoted towards gold, not RMB.

RMB's share across the functions of trade payments and financing fares only slightly better in contrast to the country's importance in the global economy (17 per cent of global GDP in current US dollar terms) and international trade (10 per cent global share). The RMB accounts for 4.7 per cent of all payments recorded through the SWIFT system; 2.4 per cent of all cross-border loans; and 0.8 per cent of international debt outstanding. The RMB is involved in 6.9 per cent of all currency exchanges.[5;6]

Thresholds along several dimensions are important for the internationalisation script (see **Table 6.1**). Reserve currency

4 Morgan Stanley, 'China's Yuan Could Become the World's Third Largest Reserve Currency in 10 Years', 2020.

5 Hofman, Bert, and Johannes Petry, 'Internationalization of the RMB: Status, Options and Risks', *CKN Clingendael Report,* 2025.

6 China, specifically the People's Bank of China (PBOC), has signed 40 swap line agreements with central banks, totalling US$612 billion.

status is, in practice, first and foremost, about acceptance by other countries of the *attributes* of the economy standing behind the currency (notion of 'reliable custodian'); it is contingent upon an *operating system*, in which commercial stature is only one component. A glimpse behind this reflection can help to put forward explanations, beyond those already well documented, for why there has not been more progress.

Confronting a somewhat unusual and unfashionable—politically incorrect but not misplaced—classification of (pre)conditions is required to sharpen focus beyond, but not wholly substitute, the noise of apologetic gradualism and 'inherent characteristics' as drivers of slow progress; technocratic fix can propel advancement only so far when the control mindset is ingrained across markets (rows [d] and [e] in **Table 6.1**). Infatuation with five-year plans where (indicative) targets are presented for the 'system' to align and accomplish smacks of illiberalism rather than faith in price signals and the incentives inherent in them.

As a sidebar, while there is much discussion and hand wringing about the level of US government debt, it is noteworthy that China's general government debt is projected to increase sharply from 88.3 per cent of GDP in 2024 to 116 per cent of GDP in 2030;[7] a dynamic not to be sniffed at—an outcome of incessant pump priming amidst centralised governance to maintain headline growth. Then there are contingent (fiscal) liabilities on account of government ownership of banks; the quantum of non-performing assets in the real estate sector have likely not peaked because China's

7 International Monetary Fund, *Fiscal Monitor*, April 2025.

housing market is yet to find its floor. Capital infusion could become necessary.

Table 6.1: Summary Assessment of Attributes, Thresholds and Progress

(a) Super hard	Share in global trade and GDP. *(Commercial stature is mission accomplished)*
(b) Hard	Acceptance is about two-way flows—a domestic constituency for both inflow and outflow of capital engenders trustworthiness in the capital accountability convertibility (CAC) policy. Capital account liberalisation for *both* residents and foreigners is crucial for skin in the game credibility.[8] Exchange rate flexibility. Share of RMB in both assets and liabilities held by foreigners (excluding low-income countries entrapped in BRI-related debt). Diverse and significant holdings provide market depth and impart endogenous liquidity. General government debt is projected to increase sharply. *(Progress is stalled)*

8 China has been gradually opening its bond market to foreign investors through programmes like Bond Connect and inclusion in global bond indices, but foreign participation remains limited—like much else, this process has been gradual and subject to geopolitical considerations. Foreign holdings of Chinese government bonds are relatively low compared to many other major economies. As of recent data, foreigners hold approximately 2–3 per cent of China's total outstanding government debt.

(c) Soft	Payments infrastructure; trading platforms; development of onshore capital and financial markets.[9] *(Considerable progress)*
(d) Super soft (and super difficult because it is, in part, about mindsight)	Shedding centralised governance. Authorities ambuscade markets—fear over allowing full play for markets-determined outcomes (the large government-owned commercial banks operations are a black box). Checks and balances, separation of powers. Central Bank independence. *(Not easy to be optimistic)*
(e) Line of sight is missing; potential derailment	Geopolitical acceptance and partnerships (some backtracking, especially visa-à-vis Japan and India, two large Asian economies). Magnanimous global citizen. RMB weaponisation will not be as destructive—for those countries that do not toe the line—as US dollar weaponisation. *(Difficult to predict)*

9 China has systematically developed key institutional frameworks—including the China Foreign Exchange Trade System (CFETS), the China Interbank Bond Market (CIBM), the Cross-border Interbank Payment System (CIPS) and the Shanghai Futures Exchange (SHFE)—which collectively provide the operational foundation necessary for international RMB utilisation across payment systems, investment channels and funding mechanisms (Hofman, Bert, and Johannes Petry, 'Internationalization of the RMB: Status, Options and Risks', *CKN Clingendael Report,* 2025.).

Against the mirror of the above classification, for China to attain the relevant thresholds, the distance becomes apparent.

Take, for example, outward investment by Chinese citizens. The summary below shows little progress when it comes to CAC:

Timeline of China's Capital Controls (2010–2025)

2010–2014 (Relatively Stable Period): China maintained a closed capital account policy throughout this period, where companies, banks, and individuals were not allowed to move money in or out of the country except under strict rules. The annual limit for individual foreign exchange purchases was established at approximately US$50,000 per person.

2015–2016 (Significant Tightening): This period marked a major shift toward stricter controls due to capital flight pressures and devaluation concerns.[10] By early 2017, new rules on overseas currency transfers were implemented, with banks telling customers that purchases of foreign currency for property, securities, and life insurance were not allowed.

2017–2022 (Continued Restrictions): Chinese foreign exchange rules continued to cap individual conversions at approximately US$50,000 annually and restricted direct RMB transfers abroad without prior approval from State

10 Patel, Urjit R., 'Managing the Financial Sector in China', Presentation as Invited Speaker at the Macroprudential Policy Conference, Riksbank, Stockholm, 2016.

Administration of Foreign Exchange (SAFE); enforcement became much stricter. A quote from Reuters reporting on a Xinhua story in 2017 is indicative:[11]

> China's new rules on overseas currency transfers are not capital controls, the official Xinhua news agency reported, even as some banks told customers that purchases of foreign currency for property, securities and life insurance were not allowed.

2022 (Further Restrictions): In June 2022, new amendments restricted Chinese nationals from participating in certain stock connect programmes between mainland China and Hong Kong, limiting investment options for Chinese citizens.

2023 (Selective Relaxation): In September 2023, China allowed foreigners in Shanghai and Beijing to move money freely into and out of the country, although this primarily benefited foreign investors rather than Chinese citizens.

2024–2025 (Current Status): The US$50,000 annual limit for foreign exchange purchases remains in effect for both Chinese citizens and foreign individuals, with documentation required for all transactions.

It is not wholly unfair to observe that the internationalisation of the RMB lacks a compelling depiction when examined through actual (gross) financial flows, that is, the lens of CAC. Hong Kong's role is indispensable to this process—without it, RMB internationalisation would merit less discussion.

---

11 'China's New Rules on Yuan Transfers Are Not Capital Controls – Xinhua', *Reuters*, 2 January 2017.

Hong Kong serves as China's primary gateway to legitimacy within the established global financial system, providing the institutional framework and market access that makes RMB internationalisation appear viable on the world stage (see, for example, Farrington, 2025).[12]

Not only are outcomes regarding China's external-facing and exchange rate policies short of the set of preconditions for an international currency, the progress over the last decade or so has been, if not glacial, too little to be materially discernible. Foreign interest in RMB assets is still disproportionately reliant on shifts of interest differentials for holdings. This is surprising and requires hypotheses to be put forward.

There are two explanations for lack of progress even as the size of the Chinese economy closes in on US$20 trillion (US$6.1 trillion in 2010, and US$11.3 trillion in 2016, the year in which RMB was included in the SDR basket). First, reluctance to shed exchange rate stability and real exchange rate targeting as an instrument for mercantilist goals (export-led growth). Secondly, failure to recognise that volatility (and market signals) has (have) to be embraced to (learn to) better manage it (them), otherwise, rigid thinking creeps in with *controls* as the instrument of choice for the first line of defence. Minimising volatility cannot be an end in itself, as, *inter alia*, it undermines allocative efficiency and creates moral hazard amongst economic stakeholders. On the former, allowing savers to diversify their savings portfolio—cross-border inter-temporal trading and cross-border risk-

12 Farrington, Mark, 'Buyer Beware Warnings on China's Yuan Push in Africa', *Dollar Watchtower*, 17 July 2025, https://tinyurl.com/bde837et. Accessed on 10 September 2025.

trading—by a liberal capital account policy could have the salutary effect of engendering confidence (ease risk aversion) and boost consumption.

Debt trap diplomacy,[13] or, pure debt entrapment?

Is RMB internationalisation more than a case of 'Give me your poor, your highly indebted yearning to borrow more and breathe free of Western sanctions'?[14]

On balance, it is more.

An important prerequisite for achieving RMB internationalisation rests upon the establishment of the institutional architecture necessary to facilitate cross-border monetary utilisation. China's initiatives for an interconnected network of financial frameworks designed to enable RMB deployment across payment systems, investment vehicles, and financing mechanisms have been impressive. A significant institutional development pattern whereby the emergent network demonstrates a pronounced orientation toward developing economies underpinned by, to an appreciable extent, unsustainable levels of development loans for BRI projects. The geographical and economic alignment suggests a deliberate positioning of RMB internationalisation efforts that prioritises engagement with emerging and frontier markets rather than established advanced economies and competitors in the neighbourhood.

---

13 Green, Mark A., 'Debt Distress on the Road to "Belt and Road"', *Wilson Center*, 2024.

14 The discerning reader will notice the paraphrasing of the inscription on the Statue of Liberty.

Rules-based system in the international finance and currency spheres—cast in stone, written on paper, or, otherwise—can only be judged by conduct and practice.[15] Non-cooperation is a form of financial weaponisation that the world is already familiar with. China's conduct—hold-out and case-by-case insistence—in debt restructuring for low-income developing countries has been less than that of an exemplary global citizen, even as it has provided development finance with commercial-rates covenants.[16] The scale and volatility of these payment flows underscore the significant role Chinese lending has played in developing country finance over the past decade, while highlighting the mounting challenges borrowers face in managing their external debt obligations. It is not an exaggeration that, to an extent, the enhanced role of the RMB in global finance can be attributed to '(unsustainable) debt diplomacy'.

In 2025, developing countries will transfer approximately US$35 billion to China in debt service payments (on US$1 trillion of bilateral debt outstanding), representing

---

15 China has established legal frameworks for creditor protection, including the Enterprise Bankruptcy Law and recent amendments to Company Law. The law provides a legal framework for the reorganisation, liquidation and restructuring of insolvent companies, aiming to protect the rights of creditors and maintain market order. The most concerning issue is enforcement reliability. Gaps in enforcement of China's insolvency laws can leave creditors vulnerable to opaque dealings and malicious bankruptcy filings by firms seeking to evade payment obligations

16 The delays and growing pains around the G-20 Debt Service Suspension Initiative and the Common Framework for Debt Reduction (Joint Framework) are cases in point.

both principal repayments and interest charges. This substantial outflow is projected to continue at high levels throughout the remainder of the decade. The burden falls disproportionately on the most economically fragile nations, with 75 of the world's least developed and most vulnerable countries accounting for roughly US$22 billion of these payments—nearly two-thirds of the total debt service flow.[17;18] This concentration of obligations among the poorest nations raises concerns about debt sustainability and the potential impact on their development priorities and fiscal capacity. But to be fair, while BRI debt is significant, it is part of a broader crisis where developing countries' external debt has quadrupled in two decades to a record US$11.4 trillion in 2023.

The confluence of reduced loan disbursements in recent years and accelerating amortisation schedules has fundamentally altered China's net funding position in the bilateral development finance market. The portfolio has experienced a critical inflection point, transitioning from a net capital provider—characterised by positive net lending flows where new disbursements exceeded principal and interest collections—to a net capital absorber, with debt

---

17 Duke, Riley, 'Peak Repayment: China's Global Lending', Indo-Pacific Development Centre, Lowy Institute, 2025.

18 In 2018, Pakistan was identified as by far the largest country at high risk posed by BRI borrowing, with China reportedly financing about 80 per cent of its estimated US$62 billion in additional debt (Ming, Cheang, 'China's Mammoth Belt and Road Initiative Could Increase Debt Risk for 8 Countries', CNBC, 5 March 2018, https://tinyurl.com/4wwmad68. Accessed on 10 September 2025.). Pakistan has had five IMF programmes since 2019, underscoring its indebtedness.

service inflows now exceeding gross loan advances. Current lending volumes reflect a dramatic portfolio contraction, with new credit origination retreating to levels last observed during the late 2000s credit cycle. This represents a 75 per cent reduction from peak BRI deployment levels achieved during the 2010s expansion phase, when Chinese development finance institutions maintained aggressive capital deployment strategies across emerging market infrastructure sectors; BRI lending peaked in 2016 at US$50 billion, and currently new Chinese loan commitments are at around US$7 billion per year.[19]

---

19 Duke, Riley, 'Peak Repayment: China's Global Lending', Indo-Pacific Development Centre, Lowy Institute, 2025.

Is China less inclined to instrumentalise the RMB in the form of secondary sanctions?[20]

Crescent of suspicion and anxiety

Fear of China comes in the way of significant RMB internationalisation; after all, as mentioned earlier, the basis is the sovereign's operating system.[21] Playing hard ball—sub-critical boiling of the pot (geopolitical tension, fragmentation)—is bad economics.

20 An interesting quote, from a recent excellent report, that reflects the nervousness is herewith copied: 'Meanwhile, even China's own official finance is usually not denominated in RMB, which, according to one source, is due to reluctance among borrowers to accept RMB denominated loans. According to AidData (2024), in 2021 (the latest data available), less than 10 per cent of China's official development assistance (ODA) was denominated in RMB. This is somewhat surprising, as China's Belt and Road Initiative (BRI) would be one vehicle Beijing could use to promote more RMB use. In the case of the Japanese yen, ODA loans ("yen loans") were used to promote the internationalization of the currency.' (Hofman, Bert, and Johannes Petry, 'Internationalization of the RMB: Status, Options and Risks', *CKN Clingendael Report*, 2025.). See **Appendix 6** for recent data on currency denomination of Africa's external debt.

21 The internal political system component of the operating system also plays a part for obvious reasons, but this is outside the purview of the chapter; *see* Nakazawa, 2025 for a recent example of uncertainty in this context. (Nakazawa, Katsuji, 'Analysis: Question Mark Hangs over Xi Jinping Regime's Strength', *Nikkei Asia*, 2025.)

China's economic coercion toolkit has expanded

The Foundation (2020): China passed a new Export Control Law in October 2020 that unified its scattered export rules into one comprehensive system. For the first time, China claimed the right to enforce these controls beyond its borders, similar to what the US does.

Initial US-Focused Retaliation (2023–2024): China began using export controls primarily to fight back against US economic measures:

- Restricted exports of critical minerals like gallium, germanium, graphite, and antimony—materials essential for semiconductors and batteries.
- Banned rare earth processing equipment exports to disrupt US efforts to replace Chinese supply chains.
- Initially, these moves were quick reactions targeting mainly the US.

Expanding beyond the US (2024–2025): China's approach became more aggressive and far-reaching:

- Created a unified Control List in October 2024 (similar to the US Entity List).
- In December 2024, completely banned certain mineral exports not just to the US, but also to third countries exporting to the US—marking the first use of China's claimed extraterritorial powers.
- Added battery technology controls in January 2025.

- Most significantly, in February–March 2025, imposed immediate export controls on five minerals (tungsten, indium, bismuth, tellurium, and molybdenum) against all countries worldwide, not just the US.

Bottom Line: Export controls have evolved from China's instrumentality for US-focused retaliation into a global economic instrument that now impacts third countries and creates worldwide supply chain disruptions. This represents a major escalation in China's willingness to use economic coercion broadly.

Source: Medeiros, Evan, and Andrew Polk, 'China's New Economic Weapons,' *The Washington Quarterly*, Spring 2025, pp. 99–123.

Muscular foreign policy and military projection for settling territorial disputes[22] with more than a dozen Asian neighbours does not help.[23] Forging partnerships with India and Japan could be helpful for legitimacy in addition to the obvious economic heft—beyond the over-indebted 'Global South', and the 'Axis of resistance'—that the fourth and fifth largest economies in the world bring to the table if they viewed China as a *benign* rising power.

22 China's more assertive territorial posture in Asia has evolved over several decades, but became particularly pronounced starting in the 2000s and intensified significantly after 2010.

23 The list encompasses maritime claims in the East China Sea, the South China Sea, and land borders with Nepal, India, Myanmar and Bhutan. The assertiveness has manifested through island-building, increased military patrols, establishment of air defence identification zones and more frequent diplomatic coercion.

The graduation from 'peaceful rise' as the bedrock of foreign policy to 'national rejuvenation' starting in 2012—emboldened by the Global Financial Crisis (GFC) and military modernisation—has played its part in the slow pace of acceptance of the RMB as an international currency. A systemic role is not only about global supply chains. Inherent risks are not merely financial (for example, a managed exchange rate), but also about great-power geopolitical conduct. Comfort levels with China are important as complete contracts, and most contingent markets, do not exist in real life. Market participants care about how the Chinese authorities—government and the central bank—will respond to and manage a crisis around the RMB for the benefit of all stakeholders, domestic and foreign, should it gain wider acceptance.

The constellation for RMB's meaningful global ascendancy has not yet aligned, but the good news is that the gaps identified in Table 6.1 are 'linear'; they are not conundrums, so they can be addressed. Hence, overall, I remain cautiously optimistic about the RMB internationalisation project.

It can be argued that China has missed a turn in 2025 because of not meeting thresholds of the softer variety presented in **Table 6.1**. It is paradoxical, but the current contretemps in the US may have burnished US credentials as a country where the law and independence of institutions, like the Federal Reserve Bank, underpinned by checks and balances—including unfettered market signals—and separation of powers amongst multiple institutions of state, has reinforced, at least to my mind (optimistically), the *potential* for self-correction in financial administration and management. Matters get stretched, break, but somehow in the 'right' way, and so get remade from the pieces with critical thresholds serviceably intact, albeit with a diminished sheen.

7

CONCLUDING REMARKS

IT IS SAID that there are no endless wars, only endless conflicts. But there are endless sanctions, and discombobulation. Until recently, sanctions have not been an appreciable part of Asia's political and diplomatic history, but given the continent's rise, its cooperation and the corollaries from it have become important.

In July 2025, the US government threatened, for the first time it would seem, *secondary tariffs* (official coinage) of up to 100 per cent on countries that import oil from Russia beyond a fifty-day deadline on efforts to bring about a ceasefire in the Russia–Ukraine war; it is a threat of tariffication of secondary sanctions, backed by the EU, on China and India for an overt diplomatic objective. On 27 August, secondary tariffs of 25 per cent were imposed on India. Complex and strained relations are enough for secondary sanctions to be imposed posthaste.

The 21st century has seen a flood of economic sanctions, bringing widespread disruption and disorder. Surprisingly, *formal* empirical findings of researchers suggest that sanctions have been, for the most part, inefficacious in realising the *diplomatic* objectives of sanctioners. The lens through which the broader subject is analysed has to be modified.

First, regardless of whether sanctions have been successful or effective in helping to realise the terminal ambitions of sanctioners, it must be unequivocally acknowledged that sanctions and secondary sanctions are a sizeable and growing source of international (macro)economic uncertainty, leading to volatility and instability for many countries and touching the global investment climate.

The pathways through which economic sanctions work and cause long-lasting harm are not completely grasped and acknowledged. The relative (in)effectiveness of economic sanctions—an acknowledged 'stylised fact' of empirical researchers—combined with ever expanding sanctions and secondary sanctions can be explained by introducing externalities in the accounting, and accommodating granular intermediate economic thresholds as a gauge for conceptually defining the success of economic sanctions. (There is the additional possibility of hidden abstract interests of sanctioners that are not picked up by data sets.)

Secondly, the smog around sanctions and secondary sanctions for victims (many in emerging economies) and voters (in developed countries) needs to be lifted by dynamic estimates from impartial stakeholders on the implications, especially for those at the receiving end of curbs and threats. How many economies are affected, and in what manner? Presently, there is inadequate, easily understood, publicly available information. And the full and refined impacts—incidence of *welfare* losses—are obfuscated. Who, amongst third countries, bears the cost of sanctions, secondary sanctions, and countersanctions (including linked threats) cannot be answered with the requisite accuracy; comprehensive and careful calculations are absent.

Thirdly, the IMF should unambiguously incorporate sanctions, countersanctions and secondary sanctions as representing different—not necessarily wholly disassociated—drivers of policy spillovers. This is pertinent given sanctions are a headwind that does not subside, only strengthens over time. The continuous increase in sanctions and secondary sanctions contrasts with the current era of trade tensions, where there are negotiations, albeit not unflawed, with instances of barriers getting streamlined and rationalised.

Fourthly, the proclivity of the academic discussion on economic sanctions is US/G7-centric. A neo-colonial mindset—that it is *natural* to control the periphery's destiny—is betrayed.

Fifthly, the rise of China, which geographically straddles Asia and, through its strong ally Russia, Europe, is a profound additional facet. The land bridge enterprise of the BRI includes Africa (imaginably via the Sinai Peninsula). The clandestine support to diverse players that is facilitated by the BRI poses a form of regionally contiguous—depending on one's viewpoint—lifeline, or calibrated domination.[1]

Sixthly, tension in the sanctions arena may escalate soon as counter-programming by countries to reduce dependence on the global numeraire currency moves forward, and steps by the US, potentially under section 301 of the US Trade Act, 1974, to push back will doubtless gain momentum. A section 301 investigation would assess the impact on US commerce, presumably including Wall Street business, and determine whether retaliatory measures are warranted. For sure, de-dollarisation is a negative for the US financial sector juggernaut. In July 2025 the BRICS were threatened with high tariffs by the US if the de-dollarisation 'project' proceeds further.[2]

Lastly, there is the inevitable asymmetry (or apartheid) in vulnerability.

Many emerging market countries typically have several characteristics, not choices, that make them more susceptible to secondary sanctions, with long-lasting effects: (i) They have less diversified economies and fewer alternative trading partners, making it harder to quickly pivot away from sanctioned entities; (ii) When faced with secondary sanctions pressure, they have limited leverage to negotiate exemptions

---

1 Some commentators have put forward doomsday scenarios where direct financial sanctions and countermeasures are described as 'the next frontier in US–China rivalry' (Reported in des Garets Geddes, Thomas, LinkedIn profile, 2025, https://tinyurl.com/hd2k5xpa. Accessed on 10 September 2025.)

2 There is little evidence that the BRICS grouping has either the shared intention or the global financial wherewithal and reach to make appreciable headway in the near future.

or alternative arrangements; their financial institutions and companies may lack the sophisticated compliance infrastructure that major Western banks and corporations have built to navigate sanctions regimes ('work or game' the system);[3] and (iii) They often maintain stronger economic ties with sanctioned countries like Russia or Iran through trade relationships, energy imports, or financial connections that developed economies have treated as a stepchild.

In contrast, developed economies, particularly those aligned with major sanctions-imposing countries like the US and EU, face less risk because they typically have more political influence in shaping sanctions policy, and domestic buffers with more economic alternatives to stymie the negative fallout.

---

3 Some major emerging economies like China have sufficient economic weight to sometimes resist secondary sanctions pressure, creating a more complex dynamic than a simple developed-versus-emerging categorisation would suggest.

Appendix 1

EU SANCTIONS REGIME

THE EU'S APPROACH to primary versus secondary sanctions regimes involves several key intricacies that distinguish it, in some important respects, from US policy.

Primary Sanctions Framework: The EU's primary sanctions are based on Common Foreign and Security Policy (CFSP) decisions that bind all member states. These include asset freezes, travel bans and trade restrictions on designated individuals and entities. The EU maintains separate sanctions regimes, like the US, for different countries/situations (Iran, Russia, North Korea, etc.), with specific legal frameworks for each.

Limited Secondary Sanctions Approach: Unlike the US, the EU has historically been reluctant to impose extraterritorial secondary sanctions. Key intricacies include:

Legal Basis Constraints:

- EU sanctions require consensus among member states, making aggressive secondary sanctions politically difficult.
- The EU's legal framework emphasises territorial jurisdiction rather than extraterritorial reach.
- Member states retain significant sovereignty over their economic relationships with third countries.

Blocking Statute Mechanism: The EU's most notable response to US secondary sanctions has been defensive rather than offensive—the 1996 Blocking Statute updated for Iran sanctions:

- Prohibits EU entities from complying with certain US extraterritorial sanctions.
- Allows recovery of damages caused by US sanctions.
- Creates legal conflicts for companies caught between EU and US requirements.

Sectoral vs. Individual Targeting:

- EU primary sanctions often focus on specific sectors (arms, dual-use goods, luxury items).
- Secondary sanctions would require threatening third-country entities, which conflicts with EU diplomatic preferences for multilateral consensus-building.

Banking and Financial Intricacies: The EU faces particular challenges in financial services:

- SWIFT (based in Belgium) operates under EU law but faces US pressure.

- EU banks with US operations become subject to US secondary sanctions. This creates a dual jurisdiction problem where EU entities must navigate both systems.

Recent Evolution: The EU has begun developing more assertive measures:

- The 2021 Anti-Coercion Instrument allows defensive responses to economic coercion.
- Increased coordination on Russia sanctions has pushed the EU towards more comprehensive measures.
- Growing discussion of European economic sovereignty suggests potential future secondary sanctions capability.

Practical Complications:

- EU companies often *self-sanction* to avoid US secondary sanctions, undermining EU policy autonomy.
- Different member states have varying risk tolerances regarding third-country relationships.
- The Euro's secondary role to the US dollar limits EU leverage in global financial systems.

Key Distinction: While the US uses secondary sanctions as an offensive tool to project power globally, the EU primarily uses them defensively to protect its own policy space from US extraterritorial sanctions. This reflects broader differences in geopolitical approach and institutional capabilities between the two systems.

The EU does not have a direct equivalent to the US dual-list (Entity and SDN) approach for sanctions. The EU primarily uses a single consolidated sanctions list maintained by the European External Action Service (EEAS) and implemented through EU regulations. However, the EU does have some differentiated approaches: it maintains separate export control regimes (like dual-use goods restrictions) and targeted sanctions lists, but these are not specifically structured as parallel China-focused programmes like the US Entity List and SDN List. The EU's China-related restrictive measures are generally more limited in scope compared to the US approach, focusing mainly on human rights concerns (particularly regarding Xinjiang and Hong Kong) and some technology transfer restrictions, rather than the broader military-industrial complex designations seen in US policy.

Appendix 2

ESTIMATED BACK-OF-THE-ENVELOPE (ILLUSTRATIVE) COST TO INDIA OF START-STOP CYCLE OF THE CHABAHAR PORT PROJECT[1;2]

1 These are based on assumptions and there are necessary caveats: the 20–30 per cent delay-cost assumption in the sanctions contexts is, at best, a reasonable project finance assumption; time-value discounting is absent; trade volume estimates are speculative without actual baseline data; assumptions for Indian business margins and capacity utilisation are arbitrary; and diverse cost types have been melded arbitrarily.

2 Iran-related secondary sanctions have perhaps had the most sustained impact on India. Between 2012–2018, India significantly reduced its oil imports from Iran, cutting purchases from around 4,00,000 barrels per day to near zero by 2019. Indian banks largely ceased Iran-related transactions. This compliance was driven partly by practical considerations—difficulty accessing the US financial system and finding alternative suppliers—rather than purely direct sanctions pressure.

Direct Investment Commitments:

- India initially committed approximately US$500 million for Chabahar Port development.
- The 2024 10-year agreement involves US$120 million in additional investment.
- Total direct commitments are around US$620 million.

Opportunity Costs and Delays:

- **Construction delays**: The stop–start nature likely inflated costs by 20–30 per cent, adding roughly US$100–150 million.
- **Underutilised infrastructure**: During sanctions periods (2018–2024), the port operated at significantly reduced capacity, creating stranded asset costs.
- **Alternative routing costs**: Indian businesses had to maintain more expensive supply chains through traditional routes, estimated at an additional US$50–100 million annually in higher logistics costs.

Financial and Banking Costs:

- **Risk premiums**: Indian companies faced higher financing costs due to sanctions uncertainty, likely adding 2–4 per cent to project financing costs.
- **Compliance costs**: Legal, regulatory, and compliance expenses for navigating sanctions frameworks.
- **Currency/hedging costs**: Managing Iran-related transactions in non-US dollar currencies increased transaction costs.

Conservative Estimate of Financial Impact:

- Direct investment: US$620 million.

- Delay/inefficiency costs: US$150 million.
- Opportunity costs (six years of reduced operations): US$300–600 million.
- Risk premiums and compliance costs: US$50–100 million.

Total estimated cumulative financial cost to India: US$1.1–1.4 billion.

This does not include broader opportunity costs like reduced trade volumes with Afghanistan, lost regional influence, or the strategic costs of delayed regional connectivity. The actual figure could be higher when considering these indirect impacts and the compounding effects of delays on India's broader Central Asia strategy.

The Chabahar Port timeline demonstrates how sanctions regimes, while pursuing legitimate policy objectives, can impose substantial costs on third-party nations (of actual/threat of secondary sanctions) pursuing their own strategic interests. India's experience illustrates the challenges facing middle powers seeking to navigate (blunt) sanctions environments while maintaining independent foreign policy objectives. The case underscores the need for more nuanced approaches to sanctions design that consider the legitimate interests of third-party nations and the broader costs of sanctions uncertainty on regional development and humanitarian objectives. As India continues to balance its strategic partnerships with its regional connectivity goals, the Chabahar Port project remains a testament to both the promise and the challenges of economic diplomacy in an era of sanctions.

Appendix 3

MAJOR EPISODES OF PRIMARY SANCTIONS ON INDIA

1. 1965 India–Pakistan war: US arms embargo

Objective

The objective of the arms embargo during the 1965 India–Pakistan war was to pressure both India and Pakistan to cease hostilities. The US sought to maintain regional stability in South Asia while avoiding taking sides in what it viewed as a (localised) territorial dispute. The embargo was designed as a conflict-resolution mechanism rather than a tool for broader policy change, aiming to deprive both parties of the means to continue military operations and force them towards negotiated settlement.

Duration

The arms embargo was imposed in 1965 during the active phase of the war and remained in effect until 1967, when it was lifted in some measure, making it a relatively short-term sanctions regime. The partial lifting in 1967 allowed for the sale of non-lethal weapons to both countries, indicating a graduated approach to sanctions relief tied to the cessation of active hostilities.

Bilateral or Multilateral Imposition

The 1965 arms embargo was primarily a US initiative. While other Western allies may have had similar policies (specifically, the UK), there was no coordinated multilateral framework driving these sanctions. The unilateral nature reflected the US position as an important arms supplier to both countries.

Success or Failure

The embargo achieved mixed results. While it contributed to the eventual ceasefire between India and Pakistan, it had significant unintended strategic consequences that suggest partial failure in terms of long-term US interests. The sanctions pushed India to diversify its defence partnerships, particularly strengthening ties with the Soviet Union. India perceived the US approach as uneven, given that Pakistan had used US-supplied weapons in the conflict. This created lasting mistrust and contributed to India's strategic autonomy doctrine as a cornerstone of foreign policy.

2. 1974 post-Pokhran test: Western nuclear embargo

Objective

The sanctions following India's 1974 nuclear test aimed to prevent nuclear proliferation by denying India access to nuclear technology, equipment, and materials that could advance its weapons programme. Western countries sought to signal strong disapproval of nuclear testing outside the established nuclear weapons states and to deter other nations from following India's example. The objective was fundamentally about non-proliferation and maintaining the nuclear order established by the Nuclear Non-Proliferation Treaty (NPT), which India had refused to sign.

Duration

These sanctions proved to be long-lasting, effectively continuing in various forms from 1974 until the 2008 US–India Civil Nuclear Agreement. The duration, over three decades, reflected the entrenched nature of nuclear non-proliferation concerns and the difficulty of reversing nuclear capabilities once acquired.

Bilateral or Multilateral Imposition

The 1974 sanctions represented a coordinated multilateral effort by Western countries, though without formal UN authorisation. Major nuclear supplier states, including the US, Canada and several European nations, imposed parallel restrictions. This multilateral approach was later institutionalised through the formation of the Nuclear Suppliers Group (NSG) in 1975, which created a formal framework for coordinating nuclear export controls.

Success or Failure

These sanctions largely failed in their primary objective of preventing advancement of India's nuclear weapons programme. India continued developing its nuclear capabilities despite the embargo, ultimately conducting additional tests in 1998. However, the sanctions may have slowed India's nuclear programme and increased its costs. The sanctions succeeded in creating international norms around nuclear technology transfer, but failed to reverse India's nuclear weapons development.

3. 1998 post-Pokhran II: Comprehensive sanctions

Objective

The 1998 sanctions aimed to punish India for conducting nuclear tests, demonstrate international resolve on non-proliferation, and pressure India to cap its nuclear programme and sign the Comprehensive Test Ban Treaty (CTBT). The sanctions sought to impose significant economic costs to deter further nuclear developments and signal to other potential proliferators the consequences of nuclear testing.

Duration

These comprehensive sanctions were relatively short-lived, with civilian sanctions largely removed by 1999 and defence sanctions effectively ended by 2001. The rapid lifting reflected changing geopolitical realities and the recognition that sustained sanctions were counterproductive to broader US-India strategic interests.

Bilateral or Multilateral Imposition

The 1998 sanctions combined both bilateral and multilateral elements. The US imposed comprehensive sanctions under the Glenn Amendment, while the UN Security Council passed Resolution 1172 condemning the tests. Japan and some other G7 countries also imposed economic sanctions. However, the response was not universally multilateral, with several countries choosing not to participate.

Success or Failure

These sanctions largely failed in their immediate objectives. India did not cap its nuclear programme, did not sign the CTBT, and was not deterred from further nuclear developments. The sanctions had a relatively minimal overall impact due to India's diversified economy, nimble domestic macroeconomic management, and international relationships. The quick reversal of sanctions policy, driven by strategic considerations including concerns about China, demonstrated the limitations of sanctions when they conflict with broader geopolitical interests. The eventual transformation of US–India relations into a strategic partnership represented a complete reversal of the sanctions approach, indicating their failure as a policy tool in this context.

Appendix 4

DATA SOURCES FOR OIL SECTOR INVESTMENT IN IRAN

International

Sources: *IEA World Energy Outlook 2010* (estimated range for total energy investment); *OPEC Annual Statistical Bulletin 2011* (reported investment in upstream oil); US Energy Information Administration, *Iran Country Analysis Brief* 2013; World Bank, *Iran Economic Monitor* 2014 (estimated fall in energy investment post-sanctions); *Middle East Economic Survey* (MEES) special report on Iran sanctions impact; BMI Research, *Iran Oil & Gas Report Q2 2015*; *IEA Oil Market*

Report 2016 (noted slight recovery in anticipation of JCPOA); National Iranian Oil Company (NIOC) statement in *Financial Tribune* (Iranian publication); Ministry of Petroleum of Iran annual review (post-JCPOA implementation); Wood Mackenzie, Iran upstream investment analysis (post-US JCPOA withdrawal); Oxford Institute for Energy Studies report on Iran sanctions impact; S&P Global Platts, *Iran Oil Sector Report* (noting COVID-19 and sanctions impacts); International Monetary Fund (IMF), *Country Report on Iran* (estimated recovery); *OPEC Annual Statistical Bulletin* 2023 (partial data); Economist Intelligence Unit, *Iran Energy Report* (preliminary estimates); BMI Research, *Iran Oil & Gas Forecast* (projected based on H1 2024 data).

Iran's Self-reported Figures

Sources: National Iranian Oil Company (NIOC) annual report, cited in *Shana* (Oil Ministry news agency); Ministry of Petroleum statements to Iranian media (IRNA); Central Bank of Iran economic review; Oil Minister Rostam Qasemi's statements to domestic press; Iranian Parliament (Majlis) Energy Commission report; NIOC investment overview presented at Tehran energy conference; Iranian Petroleum Ministry's five-year plan review; Oil Minister Bijan Zanganeh's statements following JCPOA implementation; NIOC Deputy Director statements on post-sanctions recovery; Iran's Budget and Planning Organization annual review; Iranian Petroleum Ministry statements in Shana news agency; Central Bank of Iran economic report (noting pandemic impacts); Oil Minister Javad Owji's press conference statements; National

Development Fund of Iran allocation reports; Ministry of Petroleum's announced investment plans and actual spending; Iran's Sixth Development Plan projections, updated by Petroleum Ministry.

Appendix 5

SANCTIONS ON BELARUS

Timeline of the flow and ebb of sanctions since 2005

The sanctions regime against Belarus has evolved significantly over the past two decades, with several waves of measures imposed and occasionally relaxed by the EU, US and other countries. A chronological overview is summarised below:

2004–2010: Early Sanctions Period

- **2004–2006**: Following the flawed 2004 referendum and 2006 presidential election, the EU and US imposed targeted sanctions against Belarusian officials, including travel bans and asset freezes.

- **2008–2010**: Period of slight thaw in relations; the EU temporarily suspended travel restrictions as Belarus released political prisoners.

2010–2015: Intensification

- **December 2010**: After the crackdown on the political opposition following the 2010 presidential election, both the EU and US significantly expanded sanctions.
- **2011**: The EU imposed an arms embargo and targeted economic sanctions against several Belarusian companies.
- **2012**: Further expansion of the sanctions list to include more officials and businesses linked to the regime.

2015–2020: Partial Relaxation

- **October 2015**: Following the release of political prisoners and Belarus's constructive role in Ukraine peace talks, the EU suspended most sanctions against Belarus.
- **February 2016**: The EU lifted most sanctions against Belarus, except the arms embargo and sanctions against four individuals.
- **2017–2019**: The US temporarily suspended some sanctions, though the core framework remained in place.

2020–Present: Renewed and Expanded Sanctions

- **August–December 2020**: Following the disputed 2020 presidential election and subsequent crackdown on protests, the EU, US, UK and Canada imposed new waves of sanctions.
- **May 2021**: Sanctions intensified after the forced diversion of Ryanair flight 4978 and the arrest of journalist Roman Protasevich.
- **June 2021**: The EU implemented sectoral economic sanctions targeting key industries including potash, petroleum products and financial services.
- **August 2021**: US, UK and Canada coordinated additional sanctions on key economic sectors and state-owned enterprises.
- **2022–2023**: Further sanctions imposed due to Belarus's support for Russia's invasion of Ukraine, including restrictions on Belarusian financial institutions and additional export controls.
- **2024**: Continued coordination of sanctions between Western powers, with periodic expansions of designated individuals and entities.

In summary, the sanctions have progressively evolved from targeted measures against individuals to broader economic sanctions affecting major sectors of Belarus's economy, particularly in response to democratic backsliding and Belarus's role in supporting Russia's actions in Ukraine.

Appendix 6

CURRENCY DENOMINATION OF AFRICA'S EXTERNAL DEBT

Currency	Share of Public External Debt (per cent)
US Dollar	~70
Euro	20–25
Renminbi	< 5
Other (incl. local)	< 5

Source: Farrington, Mark, 'Buyer Beware Warnings on China's Yuan Push in Africa', *Dollar Watchtower*, 17 July 2025, https://tinyurl.com/bde837et. Accessed on 10 September 2025.

INDEX